The two data processing sides of our upper brain are separated by a deep cleft because they are doing opposite things that cannot be done in the same space. The left cerebral hemisphere, "Splitter", is doing top-down analysis of the important details. In contrast, the right side "Lumper" is doing bottom-up analysis of the big picture.

Since there can be only one Executive in a bilateral brain, we are each born with our Executives located either in the left of the right hemisphere. This makes us inherently either a right brain–oriented person (RP) or a left brain-oriented person (LP). This topic is called Hemisity.

Surprisingly, many of the traits found among RPs of either sex were similar to traditional feminine traits while LP traits of either sex were thought to be masculine. That is LMs (males) were more similar to LFs (females) than they were to RMs or RFs. Similarly RMs and RFs were more similar in behavior to each other than they were to LMs or LFs. This powerful new insight to gender is developed further here.

In courtship and marriage, there are four possible hemisity combinations: RM-LF, RF-LM, RM-RF, and LM-LF (where M and F are male and female). The first two represent unrecognized Patripolar and Matripolar human lineages, the latter two are hybrids between those two. This new topic is called Familial Polarity. Referring to hemisity, it was found that the "opposites attract" of the first two pairs was most common in mating.

The behavioral orientation of the Patripolar and Matripolar lineages are conflicting, and have led to historic misunderstanding and disagreements. In fact these differences can be shown to be at the heart of global conflict. The Patripolar Axis nations and the Matripolar Allies bitterly fought two world wars. Similar conflicts are now ongoing. Understanding these differences is central to terminating human violence, from the personal to the international.

The importance of this book cannot be over-stated. It holds the key to the understanding the elusive differences between the sexes. But, much more! It provides a logical basis to understand the source and how to change the continuing conflict, originating in the ancient past and continuing in the violence now gripping the world.
Dennis McLaughlin, Ph.D. Clinical Psychologist, Honolulu, Hawaii

I find Dr. Morton to be a very unusual person whose ideas are profoundly penetrating. I have followed his work for number of years and believe him to be a true genius. This book is an illuminating breakthrough in our understanding of ourselves, our past, and our future.
Michael P. Kelley, Ph.D., Clinical Psychologist, Washington, D.C.

There are only two brain-based thinking styles. Learn which one you have inherited and why it matters to you and the culture around you.
Kent Bar-Shov, M.D., Jerusalem, Israel

I found this book especially interesting because it shows the global distribution of matripolar and patripolar population groups and the critical roles they have played in historical conflicts, including the two world wars. It was of interest how this continues today in the battles between liberals and conservatives.

Eugene Nalivaiko, Ph.D., Professor, School of Biomedical Sciences, University of Newcastle, Australia

Dr. Bruce Morton has done it again!! This is a superbly written and coherent account of how hemisity can enhance our lives and the well-being of the planet we share. This book is a must read and builds on Dr. Morton's earlier treatise explaining brain functions from his expert perspective. All of you need all of Dr. Morton's book.

Katheryn Ko, M.D., MFA, Chief, Metro-Neurosurgery, New York, NY.

Also by Bruce Eldine Morton

NEUROREALITY: A SCIENTIFIC RELIGION TO
RESTORE MEANING
Megalith Books, 2011 (amazon.com)

TWO HUMAN SPECIES EXIST:
THEIR HYBRIDS ARE DYSLEXICS, HOMOSEXU-
ALS, PEDOPHILES, AND SCHIZOPHRENICS
Megalith Books, 2012 (amazon.com)

PSYCHEDELIC VISIONS FROM THE TEACHER:
A NEUROSCIENTIST'S INITIATION
TO REALITY AND SPIRITUALITY
Megalith Books, 2013 (amazon.com)

http://www2.hawaii.edu/~bemorton
includess Dr. Morton's neuroscience
research and publications

BEYOND MEN ARE FROM MARS:

HOW THE DISCOVERIES OF HEMISITY AND FAMILIAL POLARITY CAN IMPROVE YOUR RELATIONSHIPS AND BRING GLOBAL PEACE

BRUCE ELDINE MORTON, Ph.D.

Megalith Books

Doral, Florida

COPYRIGHT

MEGALITH BOOKS

Copyright © 2014 Bruce Eldine Morton

ISBN 978-0-9833417-3-4

Library of Congress Control Number: 2014912553

General subject headings

The Discovery of Hemisity: The Behavioral Laterality of the Brain
Right and Left Brain Behavioral Traits are Identified
Gender Characteristics are Revised into Four Identities
In Courtship and Marriage, Opposite Hemisities Attract
The Opposite Right and Left Brain Impacts on Culture
The Discovery of Familial Polarity: Human Genetic Differences
Opposite Human Lineages Exist: Source of Human Conflict
Unrecognized Biologic Origin of Historic and Current Violence

Dr. Morton's email address is: bemorton@hawaii.edu

DEDICATION:

This book was inspired by Kent Bar-Shov, M.D. of Jerusalem who discovered my website and relentlessly prodded me to write a book describing my published research findings regarding the differences between the sexes. At the same time by email he ministered to my difficult recovery from phantom limb pain due to a motorcycle accident in Guatemala. What a fine human being!

ACKNOWLEDGEMENTS:

I acknowledge valued members, of the John A. Burns School of Medicine at the University of Hawaii, many now deceased, for providing the supportive environment needed to perform this work.

PREFACE

I face a dilemma! What can one do when they have been given many factual and valuable gifts of knowledge, often in controversial areas, but finds no avenue to pass them on to those who could truly appreciate them? For example, the findings you will be reading in this book. The existence of two true-breeding pre-racial human lineages (Familial Polarity) turns out to have astounding and controversial implications, from the personal to the international. But, how does one get the word out to the masses, especially if these facts cut across popular traditional thinking?

I will have given copies of this book to friends and relatives, who number about appropriately 50. But, how many of them will go beyond enjoying it, to actually sharing it, much less promoting it? Very few. I can dedicate a section of my website to the book, and hope that those visiting it will see the book as something of personal value. My experience is that such sometimes does occur, but is very rare. I can compose press releases and attempt to get them placed in the public media. However, without large amounts of funding, these will only find their way to a one day exposure in some trade magazine, unread by those who could appreciate it.

Hemisity and Familial Polarity have no name recognition. Who cares about them! If I were a public relations whiz with many network connections, perhaps I could interest Opera enough to outcompete all the other books aggressively promoted by high profit mega-publishers seeking her attention. But, that is not going to happen.

There are gate keepers which must be convinced before any information can be passed on the public media to become news. I don't know any gate keepers. Or, an accident must happen involving loss of money, or life, or causing some controversy among many people before anything becomes newsworthy. Some bizarre event or unusual behavior can catch our attention or go viral on Facebook and be read by millions. Some idea that contradicts religious belief to stir up enough consternation to get into print.

I didn't realize such a huge gap existed between we as individuals and the actual sources of news; much less the hidden steps to becoming a public figure scrutinized by paparazzi. In my case, public book reviews in popular magazines or on TV are very competitive and costly to obtain, making them out of reach of the average author. Hundreds of thousands of books are published each year and then soon go out of print because nobody is interested in buying them, no matter what their content. That will be the case for this book unless you, my precious reader, become sufficiently engaged and activated to share the material that you read with several of your friends and relatives, because you see how it can change our world for the better. If you can, pass it on to a real gatekeeper. Let's have this go viral and make a valuable difference! Namaste! And thank you for your insight and understanding!

INTRODUCTION: Are These Sex Differences?
The Intimate Problem

"Ha, Ha, Ha", my wife mocked. "Is that the way you men really think?" At her suggestion, I had brought home a copy of John Gray's book, "Men are from Mars, Women are from Venus". Now, she was lying on the bed having a big laugh. The more she read aloud, the more like gobbly-gook it sounded. A little embarrassed, I tried to fit myself into the male role being intoned from those pages, but I was having serious difficulties. Soon I was laughing too.

Later, I thought "What is wrong with us?" That book is a best seller, praised by millions of Americans! I decided that I would have to read it again more carefully by myself. A quarter of the way through the book and it still seemed alien! I kept identifying with the Venusians, and those Martian men began to sound more and more like my wife.

Ahah! In a flash, I returned to the beginning of the book and started reversing the personal pronouns of each sentence with a pencil, changing the words "he" to "she", or "her" to "his". I also changed the words "men" to "women", or "women" to "men", as the case might be. Upon reading the results of my translation, the words now seemed achingly familiar. Repeatedly, the feelings and motivations of the (now) males were almost exactly those of my own. When I was upset, I needed closeness and to talk things out, often metaphorically. Amazingly, most of the responses of the (now) females sounded almost

7

identical with the often painful retorts commonly coming from my wife. When she was upset, she didn't need to talk, she couldn't deal with metaphors, and she wanted to be alone in her "cave". When I read some of my newly translated text to her, she immediately identified with the (now) female role, and the (now) men seemed normal to her. No longer something to laugh about.

Although we both were completely devoted as partners of the opposite sex, did our reversal from the usual stereotypic gender traits imply that we were somehow suppressing or denying aspects of the opposite sex inherent in all of us? After considerable searching, the answer coming back was clearly negative. No, we both had well-balanced standard heterosexual orientations. Why then, were our personality polarities reversed with those of the couples in John Gray's Mars-Venus book?

I resolved to focus my research as a neuroscientist at The John A. Burns School of Medicine at the University of Hawaii in Honolulu to find out. The results of these studies over the last twenty years, have unraveled this mystery through a series of discoveries of an unprecedented nature and of great consequence to humanity, most of which have yet to be reported. These discoveries, each more profound and sweeping than the earlier, are the subject of this book.

CHAPTER 1. Common Beliefs About Men and Women

John Gray is a family therapist and the author of best seller *Men are from Mars, Women are from Venus* (1992) and other books targeting supposed behavioral differences between men and women. His work followed that of Deborah Tannen, a linguistics professor at Georgetown University who had earlier noted similar "gender differences" in conversational style in her best-selling books *That's Not What I Meant! How Conversational Style Makes or Breaks Relationships,* (1986), *You Just Don't Understand: Women and Men in Conversation,* (1990), and *Talking from 9 to 5: Women and Men at Work,* (1994).

Both writers recognized that in the population surrounding them, significant behavioral differences existed between men and women. They further noted that these contrasts in thinking style and behavioral orientation were regularly causing unnecessary misunderstandings and conflict between well-meaning individuals of the opposite sex. According John Gray's metaphor, such differences in viewpoints were so great that it appeared as if the sexes came from different planets and were speaking two different languages! These differences, which are often exacerbated in further conversation, have poignantly led not only to marital discord, child traumatization, and divorce, but on another level, to the unnecessary collapse of business and governmental interactions.

Table 1 lists concepts derived from the books of

Table 1, Thirty Sex-Trait Differences in the Home from John Gray and Deborah Tannen

Men from Mars	Women from Venus
PROBLEM SOLVING STYLE	
1. Solve problems directly	Want empathy, not solutions, rehearse grievances
2. Rarely talk, Rarely ask	Talk often, need to be heard, talk to solve problems
3. Must achieve results	Must have strong relationships
4. Status quo: if it isn't broken don't fix it	Seek any improvement to enhance survival status
5. Quick local solutions (life-savers)	Global, slowly solve by process of elimination
6. Hate Advice, it puts them one-down	Hate easy solutions, talk toward better solution
7. Assume she doesn't need if doesn't ask	Expect help from him without her having to ask
8. Offer to help with the details, if needed	Need help with details in exchange for support
TYPE OF CONSCIOUSNESS	
9. Object oriented, invalidate feelings	Person and feeling oriented, caring, and concerned
10. Don't read minds well	Intuitive, recognize needs and feelings of others
11. Messy (thrive in chaos)	Neat (need order, are slowed by chaos)
12. Concept matching, (top-down)	Context matching to find optimum (bottom up)
13. Literal, direct, superficial	Indirect, metaphors, superlatives, generalizations
FEAR LEVEL AND SENSITIVITY	
14. Competitive, hidden, loners	Care giver, offers help, suggestions, criticisms
15. Will not be wrong (fearful: as a slave)	Can be wrong (fearless: as a boss)
16. If upset, need to be alone to think (cave)	Need to be close and talk to find a solution
17. Suppress, avoid, deny	Struggle, approach, create
18. Cool, fearful of rejection, cannot listen	Warm, receptive, want to hear, indirect, face-saving
SOCIAL AND PROFESSIONAL ORIENTATION	
19. Seek power, competency, success	Seek harmony and cooperation, not achievements
20. Like to dress in status uniforms	Change into original outfits, flamboyant
21. Interested in news, sports, weather	Interested in communicating, coordinating with others
22. Win-lose, independent, not team players	Win-win, interdependent, cooperate with others
23. Idealize fairness (wages), penalize	Idealize unconditional love (loyalty)
PAIR-BONDING AND SPOUSAL DOMINANCE STYLE	
24. Men feel women talk too much	Women feel men don't talk or listen enough
25. Men don't listen, or ignore	Want things improved, want to improve him
26, Need reassurance of her acceptance	Need reassurance of his loyalty and support
27. Withdraw, deny, check other options	Blame, attack, panic, seek other options
28. Rate gifts in proportion to value	Rates ALL gifts, no matter how big as = 1
29. Like few, big rewards	Need daily small rewards
30. Fathers discipline children	Mothers nurture their children

John Gray and Deborah Tannen, which illustrate their idea of the differences between the sexes at home. They appear to fall within the following categories: Problem Solving Style, Type of Consciousness, Fear Level and Sensitivity, Social and Professional Orientation, and Pair-bonding and Spousal Dominance Style.

Differences in Problem Solving Style:

According to this formulation, under Problem Solving Style, men are said to seek to solve problems directly, while women often are not looking for such immediate solutions but rather wish by sharing to obtain empathy about their plight and to express their frustrations to a sympathetic audience. Men are said to rarely talk or ask for information, while women need to talk to solve their problems in front of an audience that helps them think. Men primarily wish to achieve direct results; for women working relationships are more important. Men accept the status quo, "if it isn't broken don't fix it."; women wish to improve the situation. Men find quick temporary solutions to problems; women solve them slowly by the process of elimination to achieve better long term outcomes. When facing a problem, men are insulted by advice because it puts them one down to the advisor; but women hate male superficial solutions and talk toward better ones. Men assume that a woman doesn't need help if she doesn't ask, women expect men to help without being asked. Men will help with the details when asked; women expect a supportive man to help her regardless.

Differences in Type of Consciousness:
From Grey and Tannen's system, in terms of consciousness, Men are thought to be more object oriented, regardless of feelings; women are caring, concerned, and influenced by feelings. Men often do not understand what others are thinking, while women are intuitive and recognize the needs and feelings of others. Men tend to thrive in chaos and are messy; women are slowed by chaos and need order and neatness. Men use top-down thinking to match concepts; women use bottom-up thinking to find optimal contexts. Men tend to be literal, direct, and superficial; women are metaphorical, indirect, often using superlatives and generalizations.

Differences in Fear Level and Sensitivity:
In terms of fear levels and sensitivities, men are said to be lone fearful competitors, hiding their assets and covering their positions. Women are more open bold caregivers, offering help and suggestions. Men often are afraid to be wrong as it might jeopardize their status; women are confident enough to be wrong. When men are upset, they often need to be alone to think; while upset women need closeness and talk to find a solution. Fearful men will suppress, avoid, and deny the facts; in contrast women struggle, approach, and create solutions. Men tend to be cool, fearful of rejection, and cannot listen easily; women are warmer, receptive, face saving, and want to hear.

Differences in Social and Professional Orientation:

In terms of differences in social and professional orientation, according to Gray and Tannen, men value power, competency, and success. In contrast women seek harmony and cooperation as being more important than achievement. Men like to dress in high status uniforms; women create original outfits that are often variable and flamboyant. Men tend to be interested in the news, sports, and weather; women are interested in communicating and coordinating with others. Men often are independent, playing win-lose, and often are not team players; women are interdependent, cooperate with others, and play win-win. Men like fairness with wages and penalties; women idealize loyalty and unconditional love.

Differences in Pair-Bonding and Spousal Dominance Style:

The following are thought to be some differences in pair-bonding and spousal dominance styles between men and women according to Gray and Tannen. Men feel that women talk too much, while women feel that men don't talk or listen enough. Men ignore and don't listen, perhaps because women want things improved and to improve him. Men need reassurance of his woman's acceptance; women need reassurance of her man's loyalty and support. Men tend to withdraw, deny, and check other options. Then women tend to blame, attack, panic, and seek other options. Men rate their gifts to women in proportion to their actual value; women rate all gifts from men, no matter how big, as equal to 1. Men appreciate a few large rewards; women need daily small rewards. Fathers discipline their children; mothers nurture them.

Insight that Provides Focus

Within the scope of these studies, the woman were dominant over their men at home. These contrasts between men and women appear to be ancient and perhaps best revealed in the chivalry and courting of medieval days when the "knight in shining armor" competed against others to win his queen's approval and ultimate support. As the winner, she accepted him as the best available for her. He was the one who was willing "to climb the highest mountain and swim the deepest sea" to rescue, defend, and serve her. However, she needed reassurance of his loyalty by continual intimacy and communication. He also occasionally distanced himself from her to see if there were other more gracious queens available to him to serve.

With this perspective, the differences in Gray's six contrasts in **Table 2** make sense, as well as those in **Table 1**. That is, the Queen needs closeness, caring, and repeated reassurance of her knight's loyalty and devotion. She continually demands to hear that he understands, respects, and validates her goals. She is his dominant mentor and he pleases her every wish with a formidable and powerful force. Outside of the Mediterranean, this was not necessarily true.

As western civilization has developed, women entered the competitive workplace only relatively

Table 2, John Gray's Contrasting Basal Needs of Men and Women

Men Need	Women
1. Trust	Caring
2. Acceptance	Understanding
3. Appreciation	Respect
4. Admiration	Devotion
5. Approval	Validation
6. Encouragement	Reassurance

recently. In contrast to women's dominance at home, at the workplace "it's a man's world". There, he is unused to and unwilling to be opposed by pseudo-male women competitors. Nevertheless, from a woman's viewpoint, this situation is that of a dethroned Queen stepping onto the battlefield and forced to use her feminine wiles in ruthless competition with those knights who before used to served her.

Deborah Tannen describes at least 58 contrasts between men and women in the workplace in her books. Often these create a "glass ceiling" that prevents women from rising to the top. These are listed in **Table 3 a**nd can be placed in the following four categories: Private personality at work, Public personality at work, Problem solving style at work, Solo and professional orientation at work.

Private Personality at Work

According to Tannen, in terms of differences

Table 3. Men vs. Women at Work, from Deborah Tannen

Men	Women
PRIVATE PERSONALITY AT WORK	
1. Minimal speech in private	Talk a lot in private, whatever is on her mind
2. Cautious and avoidant, unless in a gang	Bold, courageous, will fight if cornered
3. Can't read her mind	Can read his mind
4. Literal	Speak in metaphors
5. Self-oriented	Other-oriented
6. Seek mentors, political, high profile	Alone, creative, motivated
7. Chauvinistic, form gangs	Thwarted by a "Glass Ceiling", not part of a gang
8. Use of first name shows lack of respect	Use of first name shows friendship
9. A beast, not physically attractive	A beauty, physically attractive, sexually seductive
10. Big, low voice, hard	Small, high voice, soft, hair, breasts, hips, skin
11. Hunter, aggressive, dominant in public	Child care, cook, cleaner, gardener, seamstress
12. Intimidate, violent, harass, abuse	Destroying witches, accuse him of sexual assault
PUBLIC PERSONALITY AT WORK	
13. Talk a lot in public	Talk little in public
14. Dominant in public, but not in private	Dominant in private, but not in public
15. Indirect, does not look at the other	Direct, looks at the other
16. Unemotional	Emotional
17. Makes claim, then negotiates	Too polite to negotiate, concerned about group
18. Never take the blame or apologize	Often take the blame and apologize
19. Confident in pubic	Not confident in public
20. Military-like, authority figures, preach	Mother bear/hen authority figures, others assist
21. Assault, interrupt, certain, bold	Humble, downplay their authority
22. Make wrong, operate by win-lose	Allow others to save face, operate by win-win
23. Act superior, boast	Non-authoritarian, treats others as equals
24. Don't care if not liked or agreed with	Need to be liked, need agreement to proceed
PROBLEM SOLVING STYLE AT WORK	
25. Complain to get things fixed	Complain to establish rapport, to form solidarity
26. Stubborn, gives orders, bullies	Non-confrontional, makes suggestions, manipulates
27. Competitive, conflictive, attack	Cooperative, affiliative, peacemaker, diplomat
28. Detail oriented	Big picture oriented
29. Independent, hierarchical, rule over	Intimate, form networks, creates community
30. Solve independently	Need empathy and collaboration to solve problems
31. Avoid asking for help or evaluation	Ask for advice, opinion, evaluation
32. Seek authoritative information	Ask others in their network for information
33. Fast, direct, temporary, superficial	Slow, goes from vague to specific, eliminates best
34. Sure of self, denies other possibilities	Allows for other possibilities
35. Problems because of lack of planning	Plan ahead, avoid problems
36. Avoid responsibility, will lie	Responsible, honest
37. Task oriented (for his boss)	Person oriented (they do tasks for her, the boss)
SOCIAL AND PROFESSIONAL ORIENTATION AT WORK	
38. Hierarchal	Elegantarian
39. Formal, rude	Personal, polite, conciliatory
40. Ignores other's feelings	Concerned about other's feelings
41. Boast, challenge	Avoid boasting, seek to establish rapport

42. Proud, arrogant, frown, lead	Humble, cooperative, smile, can follow
43. Criticize directly, but immune to it	Criticize indirectly, are hurt by criticism
44. Don't thank, don't praise	Thank, praise others, work for praise
45. Win-lose, confrontational, adversarial	Win-win, non-confrontational, can compromise
50. Formal, impersonal, sports, politics	Personal, thrives on feelings and personal relations
51. Joke, tease, attack humorously	Self-depreciating, but hurt and insulted by teasing
52. Use formal uniforms to increase status	Flamboyant style, sexy, makeup, variety, informal
53. Competitive, decisive, use of "I"	Consensus seeking, modest, don't brag, use of "we"
54. Public speakers, claim authority & order	Private speakers, allow other possibilities, suggest
55. Clout, peck order, status, control	Relationships, closeness, connections, alliances
56. Makes others wait, uses assist. for calls	Willing to wait, but directly available now
57. Get heard, often take over other's ideas	Don't get heard, creative originators,
58. Higher rank, confident, leaders	Lower rank, hesitant, often bystanders

between one's private personality at work, men keep their talk to a minimum, while women talk a lot in private and say whatever is on their minds. Men tend to be cautious and avoidant when alone, while women are bold and courageous and will fight alone if cornered. Men don't read a woman's mind, although she can read his. Men are often literal, while women tend to speak in metaphors. Men tend to be self-oriented, while women tend to be other-oriented. Men seek high status mentors and allies; creative and motivated women often go it alone. Men are chavanistic and form gangs; women rarely are part of a gang and are thus thwarted by a "Glass Ceiling". For a man to use your first name shows a lack of respect. Women use your first name to show friendship. Men are physically unattractive "Beasts"; women are "Beauties", physically attractive and sexually seductive. Men are big, hard, with low voices, women are small, soft, with breasts, hips, and high voices. In public men are dominant aggressive hunters; while women support by gardening, cooking, sewing, and child care. Men can be violent and intimidate, harass, and abuse.

Women can become witches and destroy him with accusations of sexual assault.

Public Personality at Work

According to Tannen, the following are differences in the public personality of men and women at work. Men tend to talk a lot in public, while women talk very little. Unlike their behavior in private, men are dominant in public; women are dominant in private but not in public. Yet, men are indirect and tend not to look at the other, while women are direct and look at the other. Men avoid emotions and tend to be unemotional; women are highly emotional. Men make an offer, then negotiate; women are too polite to negotiate, being concerned about their group. Men never take the blame or apologize; women often take the blame and apologize. Men are confident in public, unlike women who are not. Men act as military- like authority figures and preach; women act like mother bear, mother hen-like figures whom others assist. Men tend to be certain and bold, they interrupt, and assault; women; women are humble and downplay their authority. Men operate by win-lose making others wrong; women operate by win-win, allowing others to save face. Men boast and act superior; women are non-authoritarian and treat others as equals. Men don't care if they are liked or agreed with; women need to be liked and agreement to proceed.

Problem Solving Style at Work

Tannen's differences between men and women in problem solving style at work follow: Men complain to get things fixed; women complain to establish rapport and form solidarity. Men give orders and are stubborn like bullies; women are non-confrontational, make suggestions, and manipulate. Men are competitive, attack, and are conflictual; women are cooperative, peaceful, and diplomatic. Men tend to be detail oriented; women see the larger picture. Men are independent, and rule hierarchically; women are intimate, form networks and create community. Men solve problems independently; women need empathy and collaboration to solve problems. Men avoid asking for help or for evaluation; women ask for advice, opinion, and evaluation. Men seek authoritative information; women ask others in their network for information. Men directly solve problems quickly, temporarily, and superficially; women solve problems slowly going from vague to specific by the process of elimination. Men are sure of themselves and deny other possibilities; women allow for other possibilities. Men create problems because of their superficial lack of planning; women plan ahead and avoid problems. Men will lie to avoid responsibility; women are honest and responsible. Men are task oriented; women are person orientated.

Social and Professional Orientation at Work

Tannen's sexual differences in social and professional orientation at work. Men are hierarchal; women are elegantarian. Men are formal and rude; women are personal, polite, and conciliatory. Men ignore other's feelings; women are concerned about other's feelings. Men boast and challenge; women avoid boasts and seek rapport. Men lead with a frown and are proud, arrogant; women are humble and cooperative, smile and can follow as well as lead. Men criticize directly but are immune to it; women criticize indirectly and are hurt by it. Men do not thank or praise others; women thank and praise others and work for praise. Men are confrontational and adversarial; women are non-confrontational and can compromise. Men are impersonal and like competitive sports and politics; women thrive on feelings and personal relations. Men joke, tease, and attack humorously; women are self-depreciating, but hurt and insulted by teasing. Men are competitive, decisive and use "I"; women seek consensus, do not brag, and use "we". Men are public speakers claiming authority and order; women are private speakers who allow for other possibilities and make suggestions. Men are interested in peck-order, status, clout, and control; women value relationships, connections, and alliances. Men use secretaries to make others wait for a contact with the boss; women are willing to wait, but are directly available now. Men often take over other's ideas, but get heard; even though women are creative originators, they often do not get heard. Men take higher ranks as confident leaders; women are hesitant and of lower rank, often bystanders.

To assure myself that these ideas were not unique to Gray and Tannen, I looked further afield. **Table 4** lists similar sex differences found in Philip Huntley's book, "Dramatica: A New Theory of Story". Further, **Table 5** shows ten differences in communication styles between men and women that were noted by Psychologist, Susan

Table 4. Ten Sex Differences Listed in the book "Dramatica"

Men	Women
1. Linear-sequential	Holistic-parallel
2. Set goal, takes steps, assess	Steps not as important as are successive approximations
3. Look at purposes	Look at motivations
4. Gather evidence	See connections
5. Set up requirements	Set up conditions
6. Break job into steps	Determine leverage points
7. Seek satisfaction	Seek fulfillment
8. Concentrate on how and what	Concentrate on why and when
9. Argue issues	Put issues in context
10. Try to pull it together (top down)	Try to hold it together (bottom up)

Sherewood. The Planned Parenthood Federation of America's list of ten differences between the sexes in **Table 6** completed my search. Clearly there is enormous overlap and commonality between these lists.

Table 5: Ten Ways Men and Women Communicate Differently, from Susan Sherewood

1. Email:
   a. Men act as experts, contentious, sarcastic, profane, insulting, bullying
   b. Women support, build relationships, suggest, apologize, thank
2. Interrupting:
   a. Men: interrupt to change subject (dominate)
   b. Women, interrupt to show concern
3. Chatterbox:
   a. Men talk more at work
   b. Women talk more at home

4. Getting your Way:
   a. Men make a direct claim
   b. Women negotiate by asking questions
5. Problem Solving:
   a. Men are direct, go to a dealer or to the internet
   b. Women use their friend network as a resource ("She had heard this.")
6. Giving Compliments:
   a. Men avoid evaluations and giving compliments
   b. Women compliment freely
7. Apologizing
   a. Men avoid, and refuse to take blame
   b. Women, apologize freely and blame themselves
8. Arguments:
   a. Men are right-wrong, win–lose
   b. Women are concerned about other's feelings, seek win-win
9. Body Orientation:
   a. Men sit at angles, have little eye contact
   b. Women make eye contact
10. Nonverbal Communication:
    a. Men are impersonal
    b. Women are intense and direct

Table 6. Planned Parenthood's List of 10 Differences Between the Sexes:

Masculine	Feminine
1. Independent	Dependent
2. Non-emotional	Emotional
3. Aggressive	Passive
4. Tough skinned	Sensitive
5. Competitive	Flirtatious
6. Clumsy	Graceful
7. Experienced	Innocent
8. Strong	Weak
9. Active	Nurturing
10. Self-confident	Self-Critical
11. Hard	Soft
12. Sexually Aggressive	Sexually Submissive
13. Rebellious	Accepting

I end this chapter with a bit of humor written many years ago.

Dave Barry's The Difference Between Men And Women.

Let's say a guy named Fred is attracted to a woman named Martha. He asks her out to a movie; she accepts; they have a pretty good time. A few nights later he asks her out to dinner, and again they enjoy themselves. They continue to see each other regularly, and after a while neither one of them is seeing anybody else.

And then, one evening when they're driving home, a thought occurs to Martha, and, without really thinking, she says it aloud: "Do you realize that, as of tonight, we've been seeing each other for exactly six months?"

And then, there is silence in the car.

To Martha, it seems like a very loud silence. She thinks to herself: I wonder if it bothers him that I said that. Maybe he's been feeling confined by our relationship; maybe he thinks I'm trying to push him into some kind of obligation that he doesn't want, or isn't sure of.

And Fred is thinking: Gosh. Six months.

And Martha is thinking: But, hey, I'm not so sure I want this kind of relationship either. Sometimes I wish I had a little more space, so I'd have time to think about whether I really want us to keep going the way we are, moving steadily towards, I mean, where are we going? Are we just going to keep seeing each other at this level of intimacy? Are we heading toward marriage? Toward children? Toward a lifetime together? Am I ready for that level of commitment? Do I really even know this person?

And Fred is thinking: ...so that means it was...let's see...February when we started going out, which was right after I had the car at the dealer's, which means...lemme check the odometer...Whoa! I am way overdue for an oil change here.

And Martha is thinking: He's upset. I can see it on his face. Maybe I'm reading this completely wrong. Maybe he wants more from our relationship, more intimacy, more commitment; maybe he has sensed - even before I sensed it - that I was feeling some reservations. Yes, I bet that's it. That's why he's so reluctant to say anything about his own feelings. He's afraid of being rejected.

And Fred is thinking: And I'm gonna have them look at the transmission again. I don't care what those morons say, it's still not shifting right. And they better not try to blame it on the cold weather this time. What cold weather? It's 87 degrees out, and this thing is shifting like a garbage truck, and I paid those incompetent thieves $600.

And Martha is thinking: He's angry. And I don't blame him. I'd be angry, too. I feel so guilty, putting him through this, but I can't help the way I feel. I'm just not sure.

And Fred is thinking: They'll probably say it's only a 90-day warranty...scumballs.

And Martha is thinking: Maybe I'm just too idealistic, waiting for a knight to come riding up on his white horse, when I'm sitting right next to a perfectly good person, a person I enjoy being with, a person I truly do care about, a person who seems to truly care about me. A person who is in pain because of my self-centered, schoolgirl romantic fantasy.

And Fred is thinking: Warranty? They want a warranty? I'll give them a warranty. I'll take their warranty and stick it right up their...

"Fred," Martha says aloud.

"What?" says Fred, startled.

"Please don't torture yourself like this," she says, her eyes beginning to brim with tears. "Maybe I should never have...oh dear, I feel so..."(She breaks down, sobbing.)

"What?" says Fred.

"I'm such a fool," Martha sobs. "I mean, I know there's no knight. I really know that. It's silly. There's no knight, and there's no horse."

"There's no horse?" says Fred.

"You think I'm a fool, don't you?" Martha says.

"No!" says Fred, glad to finally know the correct answer.

"It's just that...it's that I...I need some time," Martha says.

(There is a 15-second pause while Fred, thinking as fast as he can, tries to come up with a safe response. Finally he comes up with one that he thinks might work.)

"Yes," he says. (Martha, deeply moved, touches his hand.)

"Oh, Fred, do you really feel that way?" she says.

"What way?" says Fred.

"That way about time," says Martha.

"Oh," says Fred. "Yes." (Martha turns to face him and gazes deeply into his eyes, causing him to become very nervous about what she might say next, especially if it involves a horse. At last she speaks.)

"Thank you, Fred," she says.

"Thank you," says Fred.

Then he takes her home, and she lies on her bed, a conflicted, tortured soul, and weeps until dawn, whereas when Fred gets back to his place, he opens a bag of Doritos, turns on the TV, and immediately becomes deeply involved in a rerun of a college basketball game between two South Dakota junior colleges that he has never heard of. A tiny voice in the far recesses of his mind tells him that something major was going on back there in the car, but he is pretty sure there is no way he would ever understand what, and so he figures it's better if he doesn't think about it.

The next day Martha will call her closest friend, or perhaps two of them, and they will talk about this situation for six straight hours. In painstaking detail, they will analyze everything she said and everything he said, going over it time and time again, exploring every word, expression, and gesture for nuances of meaning, considering every possible ramification.

They will continue to discuss this subject, off and on, for weeks, maybe months, never reaching any definite conclusions, but never getting bored with it either.

Meanwhile, Fred, while playing racquetball one day with a mutual friend of his and Martha's, will pause just before serving, frown, and say: "Norm, did Martha ever own a horse?"

And that's the difference between men and women.

These overlapping comparisons between the sexes ring true for a large number of people. Yet I must emphasize that after testing thousands of people, I found they were as alien to another substantial group of the global population as they were for me and my wife, as described in the Introduction of this book. Some men were not necessarily the aggressive seemingly egotistical persons depicted in **Table 3**, and some women could very well be.

In the next chapter, I will describe a surprising paradigm shift in thinking regarding these differences, which accidentally occurred as an unexpected by-product from a new treatment for epilepsy. This new context opened the way to explain traditional sex differences in a manner based upon differences in the brain.

CHAPTER 2. Fits, Split-Brains, and the Rise and Fall of Hemisphericity

Chaos on the Ground

Suddenly, hesitating while we were crossing a busy street on our way to lunch, my dear friend, Paul, fell like a stone headlong to the ground, whacking his head on the pavement with an ominous "clunk". His mindless body began to thrash wildly, kicking, and shrieking. People passing by were transfixed and panic stricken. His face was blue. Red foam drooled from his mouth. He had bitten his tongue and was gasping. He had messed in his pants and a puddle of urine was forming. I was terrified!

Paul was gripped by what is medically called a grand mal seizure. After a couple of endless minutes had passed, he stopped thrashing and lay in an unmoving heap in the middle of the street, breathing heavily. It was over. Finally coming to my senses, I helped my friend to the curb. As he became aware of his surroundings, we began a halting conversation until Paul was back to being Paul, like awakening from a spell. Statistics show that brain damage usually occurs if such a seizure lasts more than 5 minutes. About one in five people will die within 30 days of having a status-epilepticus seizure, a rare event. Alarmingly for Paul and I, if a seizure had occurred a few minutes earlier while he was driving us to lunch, the auto wreck could have been catastrophic!

As might be expected from this human tragedy, there has long been an urgent cry for medical science to find a way to prevent these horrible seizures. Slowly relevant facts have been assembled. Paul first hesitated while he experienced a pre-fit aura during which time a storm was brewing from a small hyper-excitable spot in one of his cerebral hemispheres. As the resulting neural tempest gathered, it began to cross over his corpus callosum, the neural bridge between the two hemispheres, into the other yet-uninvolved side of his brain. There the excitation festered and magnified over the following seconds, overwhelming and replacing ongoing normal brain activities with random paroxysms of undirected mindless explosive activity, bringing Paul to an abrupt halt. Fortunately, the ancient vital activities controlling his heart and lungs still functioned in his brain stem beneath the raging neural storm above.

Splitting the Brain to Stop the Chaos

Once that it was discovered that a small neural irritation on one side of the brain sparked the wildfire of excitation spreading to the entire upper brain, it was only a matter of time before someone would think of a way to create a firebreak to block that spread. The idea was to prevent the excitation from crossing into the other cerebral hemisphere by cutting the midline corpus callosum, the major bridge between the hemispheres. This was a radical approach. Imagine opening the skull on the top of the head of a person who suffers from epilepsy, cutting the connection between the two hemispheres, and then closing the wound again. That daring thinking on the part of neurosurgeons in the 1960s, resulted in a Nobel Prize to one of them, Roger Sperry of California Institute of

Technology, in 1981. Cutting the corpus callosum hemispheric bridge by a surgical procedure, called a commissurotomy, actually succeed in preventing grand mal seizures, much to the salvation of many formerly doomed epileptics. It is occasionally still in use today.

Two Minds in One Head

However, the Nobel Prize was not awarded to Sperry for his salvation from the epileptic's curse. Rather, it was given for an altogether unexpected discovery, one which also provides a key to unlock our understanding of the elusive behavioral differences between the sexes. This discovery was based on the strange differences in the "split-brain" persons produced by the surgical separation of the two halves of the brain. After a few months, the behavior of these patients became so normal that it was next to impossible to tell them apart from anyone else. However, during the first weeks after the surgery, they were plagued with bizarre, seemingly inexplicable behavior. It was as if there were two persons with two different realities occupying the same body, one kind of mind controlling the right side and another controlling the left.

For example, one patient tried to pull his pants up with one hand, while his other hand tried to pull them down. Another split-brain patient reached with one hand into her closet for a certain dress to wear, but her other hand kept putting it back and reaching for another apparently more desirable one. One patient found that each time he lit a cigarette with one hand, the other would grab the cigarette and put it out. Another would grab forbidden food from the refrigerator with one hand, being resisted by the other. One, while enjoying a TV show, would find his other hand changing the channel. Another, while on a walk, could not go further, because his other leg would only walk toward home. A man had to stop driving because one of his hands would grab the steering wheel and try to change direction. One woman, oversleeping one morning, was awakened by being forcibly being slapped in the face by one of her hands. Conflicts between hands have also been reported regarding opening or closing a door, folding or unfolding of a sheet. One person found that he could no longer read, because one of his hands forcefully closed his book. Another was embarrassed at a check-out stand because one of his hands grabbed away the money that he was offering the cashier.

A split-brain patient grabbed his wife forcefully with one hand, while the other hand tried to rescue her. A different patient used one hand to hit his wife on different occasions, apologizing profusely afterward saying it was his other hand, and not himself that struck her. One patient developed such a hatred for one of his hands that he would strike it. His hands were observed in an actual physical struggle. Such behaviors went so far that in one case a split-brain patient tried to strangle himself with one hand, while restraining it with the other. In all cases, it was the right brain-directed left hand that caused the problems.

After a few months, these two internal entities ultimately resolved their differences and somehow learned to cooperate in unity. It has been thought that these differences between the sides of the brain normally do not occur because the corpus callosum bridging them is primarily inhibitory in nature, and that cutting it temporarily uncovers and releases our two different natures.

Roger Sperry, with graduate student Michael Gazzaniga, went on to confirm that each side of the brain had a separate and different consciousness. When they developed biophysical channels to talk separately with each side, they found that usually language was located in the left hemisphere. However, the right hemisphere could also understand language and that understanding was demonstrated by use of several clever non-language methods, including recognition of objects felt by the hand that were kept outside of view. Often, the same question posed separately to each hemisphere received quite different answers, in keeping with the independent behaviors of the hands, so dramatically seen shortly after the epileptic's brain was surgically split.

How Our Two Minds Differ

The differences between the hemispheres was later found to be based upon the very reason the hemispheres were kept separate in the first place. They do opposite things that cannot be done in the same space. This is why there is a deep cleft separating them from front to back. Thus, the left cerebral hemisphere is a top-down data processor that thrives on understanding important details. It's focus is upon the separate trees in the woods. In contrast, the right hemisphere has quite a different perspective. It is a bottom-up processor who's goal is to see how things fit together into the big picture. It sees forests rather than the individual trees. Such is reflected in the local, convergent wiring pattern of the left verses the divergent, distributed wiring of the right hemisphere.

Thus, in a right hemisphere stroke, there is a neglect of the left foreground visual field. This is manifest when the victim is asked to draw the picture of a daisy or the face of a clock. They leave out the petals or numbers on the left side, and can't draw them in. In contrast, right neglect is rare in those suffering left hemisphere stroke because the right hemisphere handles the background view of both sides.

Which Mind Wins: The Left or the Right?
After these discoveries of these radical hemispheric differences, one of the neurosurgeons pioneering in the performance of commissurotomies, Joseph Bogen, whose surgical procedure the author once witnesses, noticed behavioral differences between normal people that appear to parallel the differences between the right and left hemispheres. For example, some appeared to focus upon details, while in contrast others had a more global orientation. He called this subject **hemisphericity**. This idea became so popularized by the mass media that the concept of the existence of right or left brain oriented persons became almost universally well known. The book, Left Brain, Right Brain: Perspectives from Cognitive Neuroscience, by Springer and Deutch, describes the research upon which these ideas was based. **Table 7** assembles

data from their book supporting differences in thinking and function between the right and left brain-oriented styles in normal people.

The idea that behavioral differences between people might be related to differences in the degree to which they use their two cerebral hemispheres was a very appealing one, which captured the imagination of the popular media. As a result, a hemisphericity "dichotomania" emerged, with the appearance of commercial programs proposing insightful industrial applications and of remarkable personal or marital transformations. Some even claimed that hemisphericity accounted for differences in psychic ability or in one's type of religiosity. Others attempted to extend hemisphericity to explain racial differences.

These claims "stuck in the craw" of academic psychologists, who above all wish their discipline to rise above personal introspection accounts to become scientifically accepted. However, in the case of hemisphericity, their drive for scientific acceptance backfired. Seeking to be totally accurate, they had defined an individual's hemisphericity to lie at some unique point between right and left behavioral extremes. Of course, no one considers themselves to be extreme, so most of their subjects placed themselves somewhere in the middle. This made it next to impossible to separate individuals into right or

Table 7. Hemispheric Differences in Cognitive Styles, mainly from Stringer and Deutch

Left Hemisphere vs.	Right Hemisphere .
Speech	Music, art
Verbal	Nonverbal-visiospatial
Auditory	Visual
2D	3D, Facial recognition
Sequential	Simultaneous
Temporal	Spatial
Math	Geometry
Digital	Analogical
Logical,	Gestalt
Details-local	Big picture-global
Confabulates	Tells the truth
Rationalizes, denies	Imagines, creates
Stays within the data	Extrapolates beyond data
Less emotional	More emotional
Analytical	Synthetic
Rational	Intuitive
Literal	Metaphorical
Western thought	Eastern thought
Splitters	Lumpers
(Male)	(Female)

left brain oriented groups, based upon their marking of supposed left or right brain choices on preference questionnaires.

Beyond preference questionnaires, a second approach used in many hemisphericity studies was to look at differences in brain side electrical activity present in the frontal cortex during various emotional states. A third popular hemisphericity method was to observe the direction of lateral eye movements in response to questions requiring reflective thought. This method was thought to measure of relative hemispheric activation, being greater on the brain side opposite to the direction of eye movement. Differences in brain side activities were observed by both of these methods that seemed to be related to hemispheric emotional asymmetry. However, these were not found to be valid predictors of the differences within normal behavior thought to be central to hemisphericity.

After the appearance of hundreds of psychological and neuroscience publications on hemisphericity, no agreement was found. This left the academic psychologists with no valid method to either to disprove or approve of the radical claims made for hemisphericity. As a result, in the 1980s, hemisphericity was rejected as an invalid scientific hypothesis being based upon shaky assumptions and unproven questionnaires.

This led to general doubt and disrespect, and to consensus among academic psychologists that hemisphericity was at best a concept well ahead of its time, at worst no more than a neuro-myth that had been debunked in scientific literature 30 years earlier. As a result, grant applications requesting funds for further studies on hemisphericity were rejected, as were research papers submitted for publication on the subject. No scientist seeking tenure or prestige could even mention hemisphericity as one of their interests. Papers on hemisphericity dribbled to a stop. The subject had become blackballed by academic science. Recently, a further nail in the coffin of hemisphericity has been supplied by the observation in 2013 by Nielsen, et. al., that within the same individuals (n=1101) no differences in lateral brain activity were be seen by functional magnetic resonance imaging.

Right and Left Brainers Forever

Even though academic psychologists discarded hemisphericity as pseudo-science 30 years ago, to the general public, it is still quite obvious that right brainers and left brainers exist. Ask anyone about right and left brainers and how they differ. They will immediately mention differences similar to those listed in Table 7. Brain behavioral laterality is very real to them. Biologist, Richard Dawkins, created the word *meme* to describe the transmission of cultural ideas. Memes may or may not be true, but like genes, they are very efficiently passed on. Right and left brain behavioral difference has become a modern meme. It joins the older meme of the Mars-Venus behavioral differences between the sexes.

CHAPTER 3: The Discovery of Hemisity: Sex vs. Hemisity

Even the Greeks Knew

Actually, awareness of sidedness of brain function is at least as old as written history. For example, Diocles of Carystus, a Greek in the fourth century BC, insightfully wrote:

There are two brains in the head, one which gives understanding, and another which provides sense-perception. That is to say, the one which is lying on the right side is the one that perceives: with the left one, however we understand. (Lockhorst, 1985)

However, Marc Dax was the first in modern times to observe a difference in function between the hemispheres. In 1836 he noticed that victims of injury to the left hemisphere (LH), but not to the right hemisphere (RH), could not speak. Paul Broca extended this work by noting that often the dominant right hand was on the opposite side of the left sided language hemisphere, and thus controlled by it due to the contralateral wiring of the brain. In the about 90% of right-handed humans, language located in the LH for about 96% of them. Of the remaining about 10% of left handed individuals, some 73% of these also have language in their left cerebrum. Thus, by simple arithmetic it follows that the LH houses language ability in at least 9 of 10 of us. However, handedness has been found quite unrelated behavioral laterality. A left-hander is by no means a left-brainer!

For the following century, the term *hemispheric dominance* was only used to refer to language laterality of the brain. Then, a large study by Weisenberg and McBride in 1935 demonstrated RH excellence in visuo-spatial skills. These exquisite spatial skills provide the RH, not only with facial recognition, but also the ability to read facial emotions. Thus, *hemispheric asymmetry* has become a second specific brain laterality term. It serves to describe the brain side location of non-language skills, such as facial recognition. However, a third term was needed specifically to describe right brain-left brain differences in an individual's thinking and behavioral styles. As we saw above, the term, hemisphericity, temporarily supplied that need.

A quarter of a century after the "death" of hemisphericity and the consequent loss of a valid and needed third term to describe the brain behavioral laterality of individuals, at the University of Hawaii I created and published a new more accurate behavioral laterality term, called *hemisity*. Unlike hemisphericity with its gradient between extremes, hemisity is binary. That is, within this new context, an individual is inherently, unavoidably, and irreversibly either left, or right brain-orientated in thinking and behavioral style. Hemisity does not carry the earlier baggage of hemispheric competition or of the trainability-learnability of right- or left-brain styles. Thus, hemisity has restored a valid third context necessary to describe the existence of individual differences in brain behavioral laterality.

Existence of Hemisity: Creating New Methods

After the Mars-Venus sexual confusion incident described in the Introduction of this book, I began to notice right brain, left brain differences wherever I looked. This gave me the motivation to direct my medical school research efforts to find scientific proof of the existence of two human groups: those with left-brain orientation and those with a right-brain attitude. I had the courage to do so in the face of monolithic rejection of the existence of hemisphericity by academic neuroscience. I could do so because I had already obtained tenure-insured permanence at the University of Hawaii, and because large amounts of funding were not necessary for a creative investigator to do the needed work in this area. On this project, I refused to be slowed by graduate students, and went into high gear, doing all the work myself. I funded it all out of my meager back pocket, including the magnetic Imaging Resonance (MRI) studies, which normally would have cost millions of research grant dollars. How I was able to do so will be recounted later.

To provide hemisity research a more valid scientific basis, that was not based upon the preferential activation of one or the other hemispheres, I first needed to uncover several reproducible biophysical methods to measure hemisity that were independent of language, culture, education, or age. Each of these needed to divide a large group of subjects into the same two smaller ones, each of these which were somehow related to right and left brain behavioral laterality that was not based upon the relative activation of one side. Through insight and good fortune, I managed to find six independent biophysical methods that would do this specific task consistently. Five of these methods were ultimately published in the neuroscience literature over the first decade of the 2000s. There was great resistance to publishing them. I received as many as twenty rejections from the peer reviewers of neuroscience journals before I would find an editor with the courage to publish one of these politically incorrect manuscripts.

The following sections of this chapter trace the path of my progress. First, I discovered that normal subjects could be segregated into two groups by use of the Dichotic Deafness Test of my design. It was a standardized listening task involving the presentation of different nonmatching pairs of consonant-vowel syllables, such as ba, da, ka, or pa, one to each ear simultaneously through earphones. "Dichotically hearing" subjects reported more of the syllables presented to their "minor ear" (usually the left ear). In contrast, "dichotically deaf" subjects reported substantially less of these syllables when presented to their minor ear. It was a great breakthrough when I found that dichotically hearing subjects chose predominantly right hemisphericity items on Zenhausern's Preference Questionnaire, the best of the poor hemisphericity questionnaires from that period, while dichotically deaf subjects showed a left brain orientation.

I then designed the Polarity Questionnaire based upon ideas I had developed regarding the differences between right and left brain oriented thinking. It is listed here in **Table 8** and in the **Appendix 1**. You will note that I chose many of the questions for this questionnaire from the Mars-Venus type sexual differences of Chapter 1.

In keeping with its poor specificity, only 30% of the Zenhausern's Preference Questionnaire items, versus an amazing 90% of the Polarity Questionnaire items, were significantly correlated with the right-left brain groups segregated by Dichotic Deafness Test. A low correlation between the Polarity Questionnaire and Zenhausern's Preference Questionnaire has also been noted by others.

Filled with enthusiasm from this result, I next had right-handed subjects trace the outline of a five-pointed star, kept out of direct view and only seen in a mirror, as quickly as possible with either hand, using only the mirror to guide their manual circumscription. Faster mirror tracing with one hand was regarded as an indication of preference of the subject for the use of the opposite hemisphere. After the application of technical corrections, robust correlations between mirror tracing asymmetry and the Dichotic Listening Task and the Polarity Questionnaire were observed. The 250 member group of friends and colleagues were divided into the same left-and right-brained groups. I was on the right track! Those were enjoyable days.

One of the reasons Manoa Valley on the island of Oahu is such an exotic setting for a university is because of the existence of rainfall gradients across the islands. Because the Hawaiian Islands lie within the northern hemisphere tradewind belt, moisture-laden winds

Table 8: LEFT OR RIGHT BRAIN-ORIENTED?
THE POLARITY QUESTIONNAIRE

Recognizing that everyone has access to both sides of their brain, and that there are no incorrect answers here, mark the following statements True or False (T or F), depending on how well you feel the statement fits you personally.

___ 1. When I become upset, after cooling down I don't need to talk, I need to be alone.

___ 2. I tend to be introspective, self-conscious, thin-skinned, and psychological.

___ 3. I would rather maintain and use good, old solutions than find new, better ones.

___ 4. I talk about thoughts, things, or acquaintances more than entertainment, sports, or politics.

___ 5. I am comfortable and productive in the presence of disorder and disorganization.

___ 6. I find it very difficult to tolerate when my mate (or "important other") becomes defiant to me in private.

___ 7. I don't need a lot of physical contact from my mate.

___ 8. I like daily small reassurances of my mate's love more than monthly large rewards.

___ 9. I tend not to be very romantic or sentimental.

___10. I am more strict than lenient with our children (or I would be if I had children).

___11. Given the opportunity, I am more of an early morning person than a late night person.

Answer key: Statements alternated between L and R brain-orientations. To simplify, scores were reported as the number of possible left brain-oriented answers. That is, marking odd numbered questions True, and even numbered questions False gave 11 left brain-oriented. Right brain-oriented persons answer with 4 or less left brain-oriented answers.

first hit the windward, northeast shores of each island, turning them into vine-covered jungles. As the newly formed clouds travel over the volcanic backbones of the islands, enormous amounts of water falls. Passing on to the southwest, by the time they reach the other side of the island, the newly-formed clouds have disappeared leaving desert-like leeward shores that lie only a few minutes drive from the rain forest.

For example, the back of Manoa Valley, reaching north to Oahu's spine, is a place of tropical forest, huge bamboo thickets, waterfalls, and rainbows. This is because it receives 200 plus inches of annual rainfall. Two miles from the back of the valley at the place where I lived, the northern views of forest and waterfalls were terrific. Yet, at my place it only rained 100 inches a year. One could omit a lawn sprinkler system, but not a weekly weeding and trimming.

Looking south from my home, halfway towards Waikiki, the buildings of the university cluster at the mouth of Manoa Valley. There, the annual rainfall is about 40 inches. As a result, the campus is a verdant botanical wonderland including such sights as huge Banyan trees that attract thousands of noisy myna birds at dusk; the monumental trunk of a Baobab tree from Africa's Kalihari desert, and a Bhodi tree taken as a shoot from the very tree under which Buddha is said to have achieved his personal transformation in India. There are also wonderful tropical flowering trees such a Monkeypod, Koa, African Tulip trees, and red and yellow-flowered

Poinciana trees, and many varieties of colorful Shower trees.

By the time one reaches the beach at Waikiki in front of Manoa valley, it almost never rains (15 inches annually). This spot was called "the gathering place" by the old Hawaiians, in part because of its great weather, waves, and fishing.

It was in this setting that I developed the Best Hand Task, where 412 subjects drew a line through the estimated midpoint of a set of horizontal lines of varying lengths on a page first with one hand, and then the same set of lines on a second page with their other hand. Midpoint estimates for each hand of an individual showed excellent repeatability and stability. When the midpoint estimates of opposite hands were compared, characteristic and often large individual differences between the accuracy of each hands to bisect the lines were observed. Based upon the relative marking category, these individuals too could be sorted into right and left brain oriented groups, which were again delightfully similar to the groups resulting by the earlier methods.

Next, I created the Asymmetry Questionnaire (**Appendix 2**) which consisted of 15 paired statements. Within each pair, one statement exemplified a left brain characteristic while the other reflected a right brain characteristic. The Asymmetry Questionnaire was found to have strong and significant correlations with two other hemisity questionnaires, the Polarity Questionnaire and Zenhausern's Preference Questionnaire, as well as three biophysical hemisity measures, the Dichotic Deafness Test, phase-corrected mirror tracing, and phase-corrected Best Hand Test. Again, note its similarity to the sex difference lists of Chapter 1.

I further developed and published the Binary Questionnaire of **Appendix 3**, and the Hemisity Questionnaire in **Appendix 4** and added them to the growing arsenal of methods for sorting individuals and groups into left and right brain oriented categories. These have been shown to be comparably accurate to the Polarity and Asymmetry Questionnaires, neither of which is more accurate than 80% correct when used alone. However, when combined, they become very powerful, providing up to 98 % accuracy for individual hemisity. For use in large groups, only two or three of these hemisity questionnaires are required for adequate accuracy. Each only takes a few minutes to administer and grade and are comparably accurate to the original biophysical methods for hemisity that take much longer to use, and are much more complicated to grade.

In a 2010 paper called: "Left and right brain-oriented hemisity subjects show opposite behavioral preferences", I used five MRI-calibrated preference questionnaires (including the four listed, plus Zenhauser's Preference Questionnaire) to assess the behavior of 150 subjects, whose hemisity had been calibrated by MRI (next chapter). Importantly, right and left brain-oriented subjects selected opposite answers for 47 of the 107 "either-or", forced choice type preference questionnaire items in a manner that was statistically significant.

The resulting 30 hemisity subtype preference differences were present in five areas. As shown in **Table 9**, these were: a. Logical Orientation, b. Type of Consciousness, c. Fear Level and Sensitivity, d. Social-Professional Orientation, and e. Pair Bonding-Spousal Dominance Style.

Logical Orientation

Under logical orientation, left brainers are analytical but stay within the limits of the data available; while right brainers cans see a big picture projecting beyond the data to make predictions. Left brainers use logic to convert objects into literal concepts, while right brainers can use their imagination to convert concepts into contexts or metaphors. Left brainers make decisions based upon objective facts; right brainers also add intuition and feeling. Left brainers use a serious approach to solve problems; while right brainers use a more playful approach. Left brainers prefer to use trusted old solutions; while right brainers would rather find innovative better solutions.

Type of Consciousness

In terms of type of consciousness, left brainer's dreams are not as vivid as those of right brainer's. And they don't remember dreams as often, compared to right brainer's. Left brainers thinking often consists of words while right brainers thing in mental pictures or images. Left brainers can easily think on many things at once, while right brainer tend to concentrate on only one thing at a time. Left brainers are comfortable and productive

CHAPTER THREE

Table 9: THIRTY BINARY BEHAVIORAL CORRELATES OF HEMISITY

Left Brain-Oriented Persons   Right Brain-Oriented Persons

LOGICAL ORIENTATION

Left Brain-Oriented Persons	Right Brain-Oriented Persons
Analytical (stays within the limits of the data)	See the big picture (projects beyond data, predicts)
Use logic to convert objects to literal concepts	Imagine, convert concepts to contexts or metaphors
Decisions based on objective facts	Decisions based on feelings, intuition
Uses a serious approach to solving problems	Use a playful approach to solving problems
Prefer to maintain and use good old solutions	Would rather find better new solutions.

TYPE OF CONSCIOUSNESS

Left Brain-Oriented Persons	Right Brain-Oriented Persons
Daydreams are not vivid	Has vivid daydreams
Don't often remember dreams	Remember dreams often.
Thinking often consist of words	Thinking often consist of mental pictures or images
Can easily concentrate on many things at once	Tend to concentrate on one thing in depth at a time
Comfortable and productive with chaos	Slowed by disorder and disorganization
Often thinking tends to ignore surroundings	Observant and in touch with surroundings
Often an early morning person	Often a late night person

FEAR LEVEL AND SENSITIVITY

Left Brain-Oriented Persons	Right Brain-Oriented Persons
Conservative, cautious	Innovative, bold
Sensitive in relating to others	Intense in relating to others
Tend to avoid talking about feelings	Often talk about own and others feelings
Suppresses emotions as overwhelming	Seek to experience and express emotions more deeply
Would self-medicate with depressants	Would self-medicate with stimulants

SOCIAL AND PROFESSIONAL ORIENTATION

Left Brain-Oriented Persons	Right Brain-Oriented Persons
Do not read other people's mind very well	Good at knowing what others are thinking.
Think and listen quietly, keep talk to minimum	Think and listen interactively, talk a lot
Independent, hidden, private, and indirect	Interdependent, open, public, and direct
Do not praise others nor work for praise	Praise others and work for praise
Avoid seeking evaluation by others	Seek frank feedback from others
Usually try to avoid taking the blame	Tend to take the blame, blame self, or apologize

PAIR-BONDING AND SPOUSAL DOMINANCE STYLE

Left Brain-Oriented Persons	Right Brain-Oriented Persons
Tolerate mate defiance in private	Find it difficult to tolerate mate defiance in private
After an upset with spouse, need to be alone	After upset with spouse, need closeness and to talk
Need little physical contact with mate	Need a lot of physical contact with mate
Tend not to be very romantic or sentimental	Tend to be very romantic and sentimental
Prefer monthly large reassurances of love	Like daily small assurances of mate's love
Often feel mate talks too much	Feel my mate doesn't talk or listen enough.
Lenient parent, kids tend to defy	Strict, kids obey and work for approval

in chaotic conditions, while right brainers are slowed by disorder and disorganization. Often the thinking of left brainers tends to ignore their surroundings, while right brainers are observant and in touch with their surroundings. Left brainers often are early morning larks, while right brainers are night owls.

Fear Levels and Sensitivity

Regarding fear levels and sensitivity, left brainers tend to be conservative and cautious, while right brainers are innovative and bold. Left brainers are sensitive in relating to others, while right brainers are intense in relating to others. Left brainers tend to avoid talking about feelings, while right brainers often talk about their own and others feelings. Similarly left brainers suppress emotions as overwhelming, while right brainers seek to experience and express emotions more deeply. Left brainers would self-medicate their anxiety with depressants such as alcohol. Right brainers would tend to relieve their inhibitions with stimulants

Social and Professional Orientation

Regarding social and professional orientations, left brainers don't read other people's minds very well. In contrast right brainers are good at knowing what others are thinking. Left brainers tend to think and listen quietly and keep talk to a minimum. Right brainers think and listen interactively and talk a lot. Left brainers often are independent, hidden, private, and indirect, while right brainers are interdependent, open, public, and direct. Left brainers don't praise others or work for praise, while right brainers praise others and work for praise. Left brainers avoid seeking evaluation by others, while right brainers seek frank feedback from others. Left brainers usually try to avoid taking the blame. Right brainers tend to take the blame, blame self, or apologize.

Pair Bonding and Spousal Dominance Style

About pair-bonding and spousal dominance style, left brainers can tolerate mate defiance in private, but right brainers find that very difficult to tolerate. After an upset with their spouse, left brainers need to be left alone (hide in caves), while right brainers need closeness and to talk. Left brainers need little physical contact with their mates, while right brainers need a lot of physical contact. Left brainers tend not to be very romantic or sentimental, as opposed to right brainers who are very romantic and sentimental. Left brainers prefer occasional large reassurances of love, while right brainers need daily small reassurances of their mate's love. Left brainers often feel that their mate talks too much, while right brainers feel their mate doesn't talk or listen enough. Left brainers tend to be lenient parents whom their children defy, while right brainers often are strict, causing their children to obey and work for their approval.

Do these traits begin to look familiar? As you probably have noticed, a great many of the behaviors commonly linked to <u>men,</u> as listed in Chapter 1, end up being the <u>left brain-oriented traits of individuals of either</u>

sex. Similarly many behaviors thought to be <u>feminine</u> are actually traits of <u>right-brainers of both sexes</u>. That is, <u>right-brainers of either sex</u> tend to be imaginative, see the big picture, to think metaphorically, use feelings and intuition to find innovative solutions to their problems. In contrast, <u>left-brainers</u> <u>of either sex, men or women,</u> tend to be analytical, detail oriented, literal, cool and logical to preserve trusted existing solutions to their problems.

 <u>Right brainers of both sexes</u> often have vivid imagery, concentrate deeply on one thing at a time, are night owls, in touch with their surroundings. <u>Left brainers of both sexes</u> often think in words, can concentrate on many things at once, are morning larks, often dwelling in their heads. Right brainers <u>of either sex</u> are often intense, talking about their and others emotions, and would prefer to use stimulants to get up to speed. Left brainers <u>of either sex</u> often are more cautious, reserved, avoid talking about emotions, and would prefer sedatives such as alcohol or tranquillizers to calm their anxieties.

 <u>Right-brainers of both sexes</u> often are good at reading minds, need to talk in order to think, are open and public, seeking frank input and willing to praise others or take the blame if need be. <u>Left-brainers of both sexes</u> often do not understand what others think, are silent but effective, covert, avoiding evaluations by others and tend to be blame avoidant. <u>Right-brainers of either sex</u> cannot tolerate defiance from their spouse. After an upset with their spouse, they need closeness and to talk. They like daily small assurances of their mates love, and

tend to be strict with their kids. Their children obey them and work for their approval. <u>Left-brainers of either sex</u> can tolerate mate defiance, but after an upset they need to alone in their caves without talking. They prefer occasional large assurances of their mate's love, and tend to be lenient with their kids. Their children tend not to obey them.

From this now published research, it is clear that members of either sex with the same hemisity have more behavioral traits in common than the same sex individuals of the opposite hemisity do. Clearly, several hemisity traits are presently being misidentified as male or female sex traits. That is, men in general do not ''hide in their caves of silence'', but LMs and LFs do. In fact, the above results suggest that left brain-oriented females are every bit as ''private'' as left brain-oriented males. Similarly, females do not always ''rule the roost.'' Be they male or female, these results also show that in fact it is the right brain-oriented person who tends to dominate the nuclear family. The recognition of the quantifiable existence of hemisity carries important genetic implications that can bring new clarity to human behavior.

Thus, it may be seen that current ideas about sexual differences are incorrect. They resulted from studies that did not control for the dramatic effect of the hemisity upon their subjects. Current "Men are from Mars, Women are from Venus" ideas must be revised. Clearly, John Gray saw his sex differences through the filters of his obviously left brain-oriented view and those of his right brain-oriented wife.

If Most Individual Differences are from Hemisity, What Sexual Differences Remain?

If most human behaviors formerly thought to be sexual differences are actually hemisity behaviors, the question arises, what if any sexual behavioral differences remain? Are the feminists correct, that there is only one unisex? It has been repeatedly shown that the IQs of men and women are essentially equal, as are their math and verbal and multitasking skills. Their brain weight/body weight ratios are also equal.

Yet obviously, the sexes are anatomically different. Men are usually larger, stronger, and physically more aggressive than women. They have been said to have better motor and spatial abilities. They penetrate with their penises. Women are receptive, both physically and often in terms of behavioral passivity toward the stronger, more massive, risk-taking males. Women are impregnated by men and must incubate, bear, and nurse the resulting offspring. They are nurturing and seek loyalty, support, and protection of their children from their partner. Women have been said to have superior memory and social cognition skills. On the other hand, a man competes to father as many children as possible in order to leave his mark on the evolution of the species. These crossed purposes between the sexes must result in behavioral differences. Perhaps females have higher levels of jealousy and manipulative seductiveness than males. I have never found men to be as insanely jealous as some women I

55

have known. It is said that women cry 4x more often than men and also live longer.

Another clue to true sexual differences comes from the behaviors of homosexuals, especially those of transvestites. Natural body English movements and gestures, along with difficult to avoid vocal inflections often give crossed-sex people away, even when they are trying to remain in "the closet". Thus, gay men with female identities often show feminine behaviors such as the classic "limp wrist", "lisp-like" pronunciations, hip sways, prancing, and other graceful body reflexes, along with the desire for self-beautification, exaggerated in flamboyant Drag Queens, all of which could be said to be true female behaviors. Conversely, lesbians with male identities can appear abrupt, hard, and aggressive in demeanor with a tendency to wear rough attire, suggestive of male behavior.

Another level deals with sexual differences in behavior in terms of parental relationships with their offspring. It has been suggested that the role of a mother is to give their child a basic sense of security in the world, and the role of a father is to empower his child to go out and become a young man or woman. A counselor put it another way: An ability to receive (receptivity) comes from the mother; an ability to operate in the world (empowerment) comes from the father. A psychiatrist puts it this way: a lack of mothering leads to fear; a lack of fathering leads to powerlessness. A pastor puts it this way: a lack of mothering leads to insecurity; a lack of fathering leads to inferiority.

These type of sexual differences are remarkably similar to those pointed out to exist in US politics by George Lakoff in his book *Moral Politics*, 2002. There, Liberals are shown unwittingly to follow a "Nurturant Parent" morality of empathy, acceptance of differences, with assistance and protection of the weaker. In contrast, Conservatives appear to adhere to an underlying "Strict Father" morality, of enforced self-discipline, reward or punished by authoritarian rules.

The sexes appear to segregate as preteens. The play of boys is competitive rough and tumble, while the girls show camaraderie. The boys are dominant over girls and ignore them. Their attitudes and interests differ. Boys are profoundly attracted to trucks, trains, and aircraft, even if brought up as a girl. Girls are fascinated by attractive clothing and child-like dolls. These appear to be inherent, not learned differences.

Recently, it has been discovered that two hormones affect the social synchrony within reproductive pairs. Oxytocin secretion appears to influence maternal behaviors, while vasopressin affects paternal behaviors. Mothers with higher level of oxytocin provided more affectionate contact and more sustained eye contact. Fathers with higher vasopressin levels gave more stimulatory contact, paying shared attention to objects with the child.

Hemisity also Trumps Current Sexual Identities at Work

Hemisity also explains much of the so-called male-female role differences in the workplace assembled by Deborah Tannen, as listed in Chapter 1. Obviously, she is a RF and many of the aggressive, antisocial males around her were LMs. It is interesting how one's own hemisity contaminates the way one sees others in our environment. My own personal bias as a RM for years distorted my views of other males and females. For years I sought to identify with the male member of a couple, seeking his support, assuming that he was the King. Often this was a waste of time, since it was the Queen who ruled and he was only her Knight. Thus, Professor Tannen almost completely ignores LFs and RMs at work, even though there are many of such who operate quite successfully in the business and academic world. In fact, there are more big-picture RM CEOs in corporations than there are detail oriented LMs, who tend to compete within the middle levels. Also, for some RMs, there is just as much a "Glass Ceiling" as there is for RFs. I was the only RM in my academic department, containing a dozen LMs. We just did not speak the same language. Nor did my more cooperative nature fare well in the cut-throat turf wars of faculty meetings.

The demonstration that the great majority of the traditional differences between men and women listed in Chapter 1 are actually hemisity differences is now forcing us to reassess ourselves as men and women. It certainly begins to answer why only about half of the population identify with the Men from Mars, Women from

Venus model. They are the left brained men and right brained women. But why had they self-selected themselves into such marital pairs? And what about the rest of us, including my right brained self and my left brained wife? Much more of this mystery remains to be unraveled. And it will be!

A suggestion at this point: Scanning the four new Hemisity Questionnaires of this chapter into files will enable you to make the copies needed to find out the hemisity of yourself, your family, and friends. You may be interested in the results of your studies as this book progresses.

CHAPTER 4: Finding Neuroanatomical Differences between R and L Brainers

Here Comes That Corpus Callosum Again

The new methods of Chapter 3 enabled me accurately to determine hemisity subtype of thousands of subjects in the University of Hawaii (UH) community. The next big question was to ask whether hemisity was based upon differences in brain structural anatomy between right- and left-brainers. The brain contains about 20 billion neurons. The **corpus callosum** is the major tract connecting the right and left cerebral hemispheres. Yet, only 1-3% of cerebral neurons cross the corpus callosum. Those that do are often inhibitory. In the neuroscience literature I had read reports that individuals varied up to three-fold in the size of their corpus callosum. That is, one person could have an interhemispheric communication link that was three times the size of another.

Recall, that this was the transhemispheric communication structure that had been cut to prevent grand mal seizures and in the process to produce the split-brain persons described in Chapter 2. Although scientists had tried to tie these large differences in the extent of corpus callosal linkage between the hemispheres to such things as sex or handedness differences, they had come up empty. Nobody knew how someone having three times the communicating power between the hemispheres would differ from another person with a smaller corpus callosum. I felt that this callosal size difference between individuals must have something to do with hemisity.

Hospital Intrigue Worth A Million Dollars

Obviously, the way to go about finding out whether this was true was to use magnetic resonance imaging (MRI), a powerful new tool for looking inside the living brain with high resolution to see who had a large or small corpus callosum. However, such an MRI equipment package, including the huge magnet within which a patient's head was inserted, cost several million dollars. At the time, only three MRI centers existed in the State of Hawaii. The one accessible to me was under intense use at the Kaiser Medical Center in Honolulu. Normally, a well-known neuroscientist would apply for a large grant from the National Institute for Mental Health in Washington, D.C. to cover the expense of buying research time on busy MRI equipment and paying for a technician and supplies. Such a million dollar plus grant would take more than a year to obtain, if all went well. However, what grant application panelist had ever heard of hemisity, being uncovered by an unknown investigator way out in Hawaii? Such a grant would literally be impossible for me to obtain.

Yet, I was convinced that hemisity was based upon brain structural differences between right- and left-brainers. And that these differences could only be made visible by the use of MRI. Obtaining MRI brain scans on more than 150 of my hemisty pre-calibrated individuals, was going to take some wily creativity on my part!

After some thought, I hatched a plan. Brazenly walking into the hospital, I found my way to the Diag-

nostic Imaging Department. There, I asked the reception-
ist if I could speak with one of the MRI technicians. Soon
one came to the front desk. I asked him which of the ra-
diologists whom he assisted in running the MRI instrument was the most oriented toward research. "Oh yes",
the technician said, "Dr. Stein Rafto", one of the radiolo-
gists, "often discussed brain research." So far so good!

I next made an appointment to see Dr. Rafto. He
was obviously an intelligent, enthusiastic man. I briefly
told him of my hemisity work and my belief that MRI
could reveal neuroanatomical differences between right-
and left-brainers. Dr. Rafto was definitely open to the
idea. I offered him coauthorship on any MRI papers that
might result from our collaboration. However, he warned
me that he was "110%" overbooked in the scanning of
hospital patients whose individual MRI scans took at
least 45 minutes to perform, and could see no way he
could help me. How disappointing! But what did I expect!

Then it hit me. I told him that I didn't need to scan
all of the brain, only the midline where the corpus callosum crossed over. "Ah hah", he said! "We always do a
midline scan to calibrate the instrument for each patient
before making a run. The procedure only takes three
minutes!" This calibration scan was at high resolution
and would be all that I needed. How exciting! But Dr.
Rafto still didn't think he could see a way to work my
subjects in during his daily routine.

Then he had another idea. He said that he knew a
bright research-oriented MRI technician who might be

persuaded to work off hours. If he agreed, Dr. Rafto would allow the MRI instrument to be used on my project under his supervision. I quickly made an appointment to see the MRI technician. He appeared interested in the project, so I offered him $10/head if we could bring in two or three of my subjects of known hemisity at a time evenings or weekends. Thank goodness he agreed. I was in! Although it took almost a year to scan my 150 volunteers, they were happy to come in, in part because they were promised copies of their own brain scans and because of the excitement that comes from being part of an interesting research project. The only three-minute scan also avoided much of the claustrophobia that often comes with the usual 45 minute run. The ultimately $1500 out of pocket investment turned out to be well worthwhile!

Big Differences in Corpus Callosal Size Between Right and Left Brainers

What we found was that the corpus callosal size of right-brainers, whether male or female, was up to three times larger on average than that of left-brain males or females in keeping with my predictions. (For technical reasons, the figure labeled Figure 2 is the first figure presented here, the figure labeled Figure 1 follows next). For example **Figure 2** shows the brain midline scans of persons with the largest and smallest corpus callosal cross-sectional areas of the 113 subjects of this study. Of these callosal sizes, the female with the largest was a UH English professor. I ended up being the male with the largest.

By strange chance, the man with the smallest callosum was a UH dean, the husband of the same English professor. To carry these uncanny coincidences to the bitter end, the woman in the study with the smallest callosum was my now ex-wife, a physician! Clearly, corpus callosal size had absolutely nothing to do with I.Q.

Early reports had suggested that males had smaller corpora callosa than females. This was often interpreted to support the concept that male brains are more lateralized or specialized, thus accounting for presumed male predominance in mathematics, as well as in aggressive behavior. Ultimately, meta-analyses of these many reports found no significant overall sex differences in intercerebral information carrying capacity. As described here, using quantitative MRI, we found that the corpus callosal size of 113 subjects was significantly correlated, not with handedness or sex, but hemisity. The latter accounted for over 19% of corpus callosum variability, the largest correlation ever reported. That is, right brain-oriented individuals of either sex had significantly larger corpus callosal midline areas than left brain-oriented persons did.

It may be that because left-brainers have their language center in their left hemisphere, they need less cross-communication with their left sided Executive than right-brainers whose left language center is on the opposite side from their right brain Executive. Also, having a smaller corpus callosum may leave left-brainers with less access to their right hemispheres. It took fighting through many years of rejections finally to get these results

Figure 2: Hemisphericty vs. Sex:
Size-Range of Corpus Callosal Areas

Right Brain Oriented Female   Left Brain Oriented Female

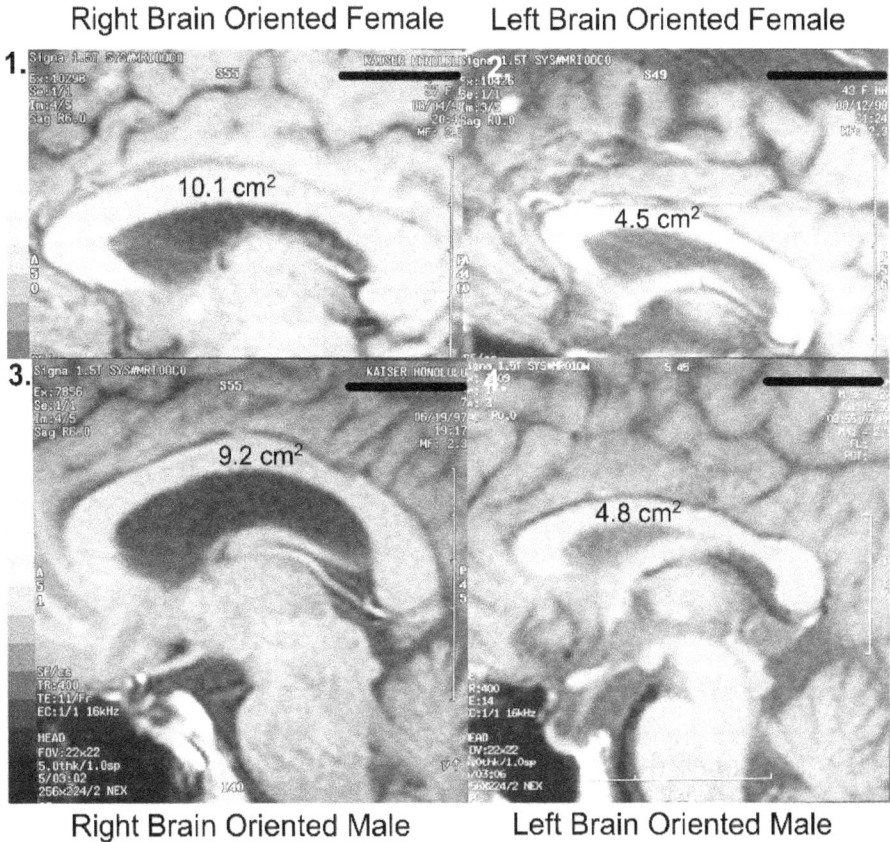

Right Brain Oriented Male   Left Brain Oriented Male

Legend: These MRI images were taken at the front (left side in photos) to back midline of the brain of four individuals of known hemisity. The nearly white, rotated letter C-like central structure in the center is the corpus callosum containing millions of nerve fibers crossing between the two cerebral hemispheres. Their cross sectional areas are marked on them. This is the structure that is severed in epileptics to produce split-brain individuals. The individuals on the left had the largest corpora callosa in the group of 113 subjects of this study. Those on the right had the smallest. The cingulate cortex, topic of the next chapter, lies immediately above the corpus callosum.

published. At that time I was still was using with the doomed term, hemisphericity, having yet to invent the idea of hemisity.

So, although it was shown that on average there is essentially no difference between the corpus callosal sizes of men and women, callosal size of right-brain males and females was significantly greater than those of left-brain males and females (**Figure 2**). This then was yet another reason why right-brained men and women have far more commonalities than differences. The same was true for the similarities of left-brained men and women.

However, these two RP and LPs groups differed in another important way. The first group spoke the "Rightese" Venusian dialect (of English), quite a different language than the "Leftese" Martian dialect spoken by the other group. Was this the true basis for all the misunderstandings and confusion! What was going on here? A review of the ten publications upon which the discovery of hemisity is based was published under the title "Behavioral Laterality of the Brain: Support for the Binary Construct of Hemisity" by Bruce Morton in the journal, Frontiers in Psychological Research, in 2013, see doi: 10.3389/fpsyg.2013.00683

In 2013, a paper by Ingalhalikar, et al. was published claiming to demonstrate substantial brain connection differences between men and women by use of diffusion tensor imaging. They reported that the cerebral hemispheres of men had greater within-hemispheric connectivity, whereas between-hemispheric connectivity was greater in the brains of women. The opposite was found within the cerebellum. They interpreted their results to show that "male brains are structured to facilitate connectivity between perception and coordinated action, whereas female brains are designed to facilitate communication between analytical and intuitive processing modes." That is, they interpreted their results to support the same Men are from Mars model as Grey and Tannen had developed, described in Chapter 1.

However, as described in the Introduction, the Gray-Tannen sexual differences model does not fit almost half of the US population, and clearly does not allow for the existence of hemisty, which was unknown at the time. The author of the present book asserts that if the hemisity of their subjects had also been measured, something that is now quick and easy to do, it would have been discovered that their model fits only LMs and RFs. It does not fit RMs or LFs, such as my wife and myself as representative of a large percentage of the population. Similarly, if the hemisity of the Ingalhalikar subjects were to be measured, it will be found that their approach will have provided powerful support for the existence of hemisity. That is, more of their men will be found to be LMs and more of their females to be RFs. In fact their method appears to be a direct assay for hemisity! If they could sort their subjects by hemisity, they would obtain even more dramatic differences in connectivity between RPs and LPs, because their subject groups were of mixed hemisity giving less clear cut results. In fact, I have implored them to do so, with no reply. Why both the Gray-Tannen and the Ingalhalikar populations appear to be impoverished in RMs and LFs can now be understood, and is based upon the existence of Familial Polarity, a topic to be developed later in this book.

CHAPTER 5: Why Does Hemisity Exist?
The Unilateral Executive Ego

A Second Neuroanatomical Difference Between Right- and Left-Brainers

Since, as described in the last chapter, comparing hemisity subtype with individual differences in the corpus callosum had paid off royally,. I began to search the neuroscience literature for other large variations in brain structure between individuals. What caught my eye were the big differences in a deep brain structure, called the anterior cingulate cortex (ACC), which importantly was associated with brain executive function. This structure is located immediately above the corpus callosum, as illustrated in **Figure 1.** It is completely bilateral, its sides being physically separated by the great cleft between the cerebral hemispheres whose depth reaches that of the corpus callosal crossing. The folds in the cingulate cortex had repeatedly been shown to have large individual differences between sides.

For me, two things were important about these cingulate cortex variations. First, because the three minute MRI calibration included not only a midline image, but also two other images 6mm on either side, amazingly, I had already inadvertently obtained MRI images of the cingulate cortex on both sides of all 150 of my earlier hemisity-calibrated subjects in the corpus callosum study! What an absolute stroke of good fortune!

Figure 1. Executive Observer on One Side of the Cingulate Cortex

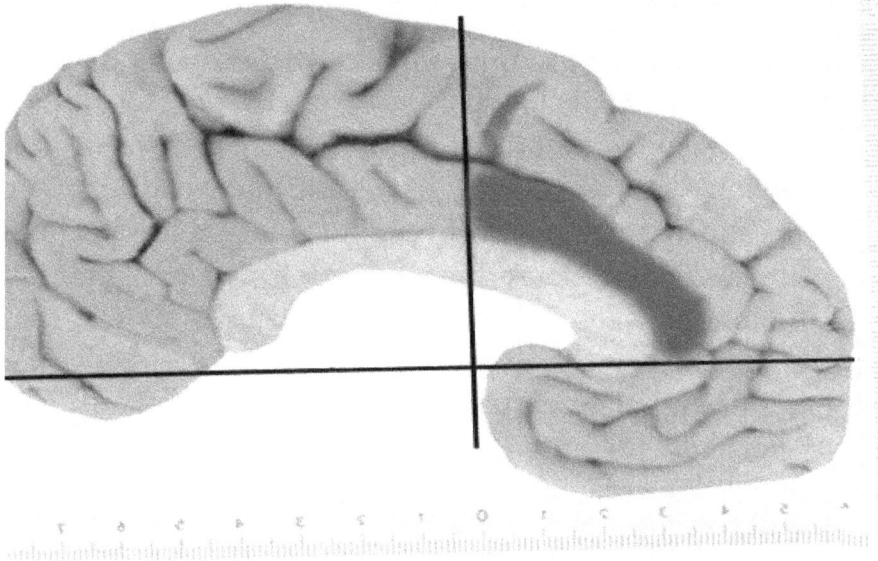

The Cingulate Cortex: A Brain Site for Freud's Ego

The second important thing about reports of anterior cingulate cortex asymmetries was that this cortical element of the ancient limbic brain region has repeatedly been shown to be involved in subconscious executive-type activities. These included decision making, error detection, conflict monitoring, stimulus-response mapping, familiarity, orienting response to pain, and production of emotion. Its published verbal and non-verbal executive task activities included conflict monitoring and adjustments in control, rapid processing of gains and losses, interfacing between motor control, drive, and cognition, episodic memory retrieval and the initiation and motivation of goal directed behavior. Some ACC activities appeared directly relevant to hemisity differences in behavioral styles. These included its participation in temperament, reward and social learning, expectancy and social rejection, self-reflection, personality, will, and addiction.

Even though Freud's psychoanalytic concepts were originally not intended to correspond to neuroanatomical structures, the ACC has increasingly appeared to be associated with the functions of Freud's Ego, whose structural basis had yet to be found. It certainly has the resources to implement the many behavioral differences between hemisity subtypes. Like Freud's Id and Superego, the Ego acts outside of our awareness. As neuroscientist Benjamin Libet demonstrated in 1986, we become aware of its decisions about a second later, thinking they are our own. These relationships fall within the realm of the Dual Quadbrain Model, another of my areas of interest.

An impressive experimental confirmation for the Executive Ego being produced by the cingulate cortex was provided by the recent findings for volunteers suffering ego death by the ingestion of the hallucinogen, psilocybin. A preferential and profound bilateral inhibition of anterior, and especially the posterior cingulate cortex was observed by functional MRI under those transformational conditions.

In the Bilateral Brain, Which Side is the One and Only You On?

I was excited to analyze the MRI scans for differences in the structure of the cingulate cortex between the two sides of the brain of my 150 hemisity subjects. Incredibly, I found that in 146 of 149 cases (98%), the subject's bilateral anterior cingulate cortex was up to 50% larger on the right side of RPs, while for the LPs it was up to 50% larger on the left. The area of particular interest involved the brain mapping Areas 24 and 24' which are darkened in **Figure 1**, This significant discovery is illustrated in **Figure 3** where the ACC size differences are readily visible. It was the second neuroanatomical difference ever found between right and left brain-oriented persons.

Why was this an important finding? Here was a new method that wasn't just 80% accurate in determining the hemisity of an individual, it was 98% accurate! I immediately made it the primary standard for hemisity. I then used it to check my previous biophysical and questionnaire methods for determining hemisity subtypes and was gratified to find them to be valid indeed. That confirmed that all of the sometimes risky assumptions upon which they were built were correct. Because the now MRI-validated questionnaires listed in Chapter 3 are much simpler to use than going to the hospital for an MRI, not to mention the cost, they can be used in combination giving over 95% certainty that one is right or left brain-oriented.

Figure 3: Asymmetries of the Anterior Cingulate Cortex

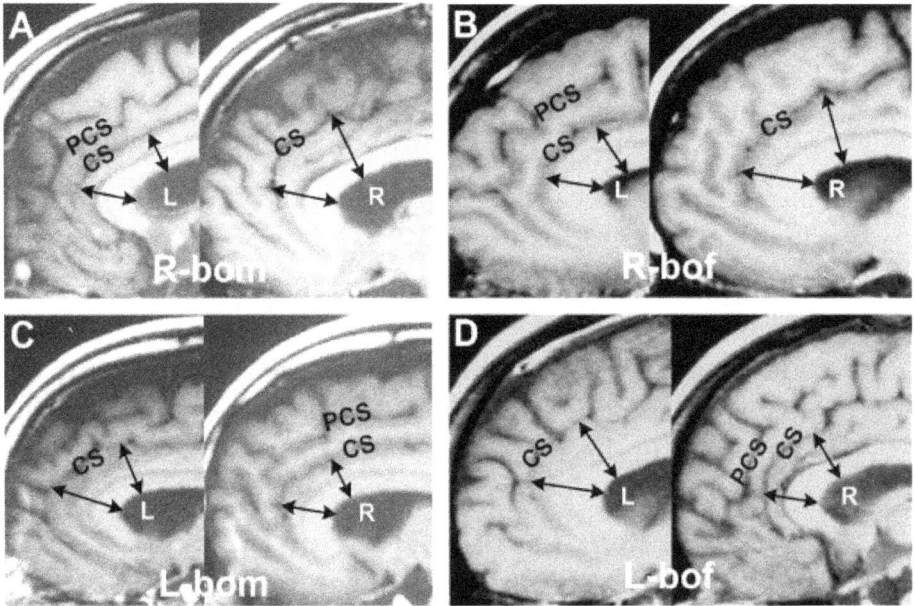

Legend for Figure 1. Example of MRI sagittal images taken from 149 hemisity-calibrated subjects. Pairs of arrows reaching from the lower surface of the central white corpus callosum to the cingulate sulcus (CS) illustrate four measurements made for each subject. Corpus callosal thickness was the same on images from either side. PCS refers to the paracingulate sulcus. R-bom is right brain oriented male, L-bom is left brain-oriented female, etc. Note that the arrow lengths are longer on the right side for right brain-oriented persons and on left side for left brain –oriented persons.

Although, these were important advances for hemisity, by far the most important conclusion from these MRI results was evidence that our Executive Ego is unilateral. That is, it resides on one side of the brain or the other in an individually idiosyncratic (variable) manner. To explain this, consider the following: In any institution, including that of the brain, there can be only one executive, chief, bottom-line, "the buck stops here" responsible final cause. Since all mammalian brains, including those of humans have two sides, the question becomes: Which side are You on?! What this discovery tells us is that if your Executive Ego is imbedded in your right hemisphere, you will be a bottom-up, big picture, lumper, i.e., a right brain-oriented person (RP), male (RM) or female (RF) as the case may be. If it was born on the left side, your Executive Ego will be a top-down, important details, splitter and you are a left brain-oriented person (LP), either male (LM) or female (LF).

A Confirmation: There is Only One Observer

Just to be sure of these conclusions, I designed another way to test them. I invented a new kind of instrument, called a hemisometer, to see if our inner observer was really only to be found on one side of our brain. Using the flash hemisometers illustrated in **Figure 4,** a single 0.5 millisecond was directed to each cerebral hemisphere simultaneously via both nasal, or both temporal retinal surfaces. These terms are needed because each of the retinae of our eyes are bilateral with the retinal half on the side of one's temple going to one side of the brain and the nasal half on the side of the nose going to the other brain side. Because of this ingenious wiring, if one loses one eye, visual inputs from the other eye will still go to both sides of the brain.

**Figure 4: Flash Hemisometer Design and Function, Illustrated
by a Subject with their Executive Observer on the Left**

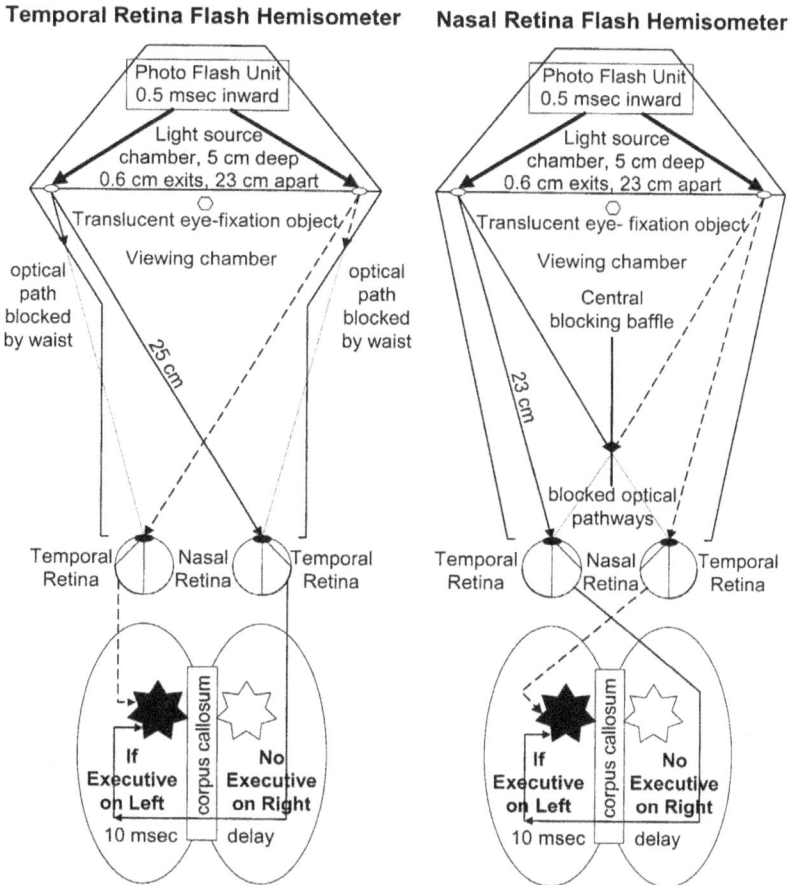

Figure 5 shows my son, Dan, using a hemisometer.

Now grasp this! From a <u>single</u> flash simultaneously directed to each brain side, 87 of my 91 subjects (95%) reported <u>two</u> flashes! What was going on here?! The first flash was seen on one side, closely followed by a second flash on the same side. Further, which side saw the flashes first turned out to be the side of the subject's hemisity! Elegant, if I do say so myself. The simplest explanation was that the brain side seeing the first flash was the one containing the subject's executive observer. The light simultaneously flashed to the other side could not be seen there, because the sole observer was not on that side. However, that flash was then shunted across the corpus callosum with a time delay to the observer on the first side to be noted as the closely following second flash.

These results confirmed that there was only one observer and that it was on the same side as the subject's hemisity. After submission to many journals, I have been unable to get these results published.

Further Hemisity Differences Beyond Behavior

So what could it mean if in each of us our unconscious Executive Ego was born either on the right or left side of our brains in an unknown manner? Clearly, people whose executive is imbedded within the top-down processing left hemisphere must see things differently than those whose executive is located on the right, bottom-up processor. Further, there were other yet unproven differences that had anecdotally been observed,

Figure 5: Photo of Flash Hemisometer in Use.

some of which are listed in **Table 10.** These go beyond thinking-style differences to include several additional differences in propensities, health, and even some physical ones.

Table 10 may be understood as follows: In terms of personality, left brainers are sensitive while right brainers are more intense. In keeping with this, left brainers prefer unseasoned food in contrast to right brainers

Table 10. Other Differences Between Hemisity Subtypes: Anecdotal

Issue:	LPs:	RPs:
Personality Type:	High sensitivity	High intensity
Taste:	Prefer unseasoned	Prefer spicy
Smell:	Aroma sensitive	Odor: less sensitive
Stress:	Vulnerable	Resistant
Basal Fear:	Anxious	Bold
Dream content:	Monsters, Falling	Humiliation, Excreta
Drugs of abuse:	Relaxants (alcohol)	Stimulants (amphet.)
Immune strength:	Weak	Strong
Proneness to Illness:	Often ill	Rarely ill
Medicine side effects:	Common	Uncommon
Proneness to Obesity:	Often thin	Often overweight
Bust size:	Smaller	Larger
Non-erect penis length	Long	Short
Longevity:	Type A mortality	Youthful
Mental Health issues	Alcoholism, PTSD	Dyslexia

who love spicy food. Left brainers have a sensitive sense of smell, while right brainers often do not. Left brain sensitivity makes them more vulnerable to stress and anxiety than right brainers who are more stress resistant and bold. Often left brainers dream of monsters or of falling, while dreams of right brainers may be humiliating or contain excrecia. In terms of drugs of abuse, overanxious lefts prefer relaxants such as alcohol to get down to the "good" zone, while overly calm right brainers tend to prefer stimulants, such as amphetamines to get up to it.

Sensitive left brainers have lower immune strength and often are ill, while intense right brainers have higher immune defenses and are rarely ill. Left brain sensitivity leave them more vulnerable to side effects of medicines than right brainers. Left brainers usually are thinner than right brainers. Left brain women breasts are often smaller than those of right brain women. The non-erect penis length of left brainers is substantially longer than that of right brainers whose penises can shrink substantially when not erect. Left brainers are more subject to stress illnesses such as heart attacks and cancer than right brainers who tend to look more youthful. Left brainers are more vulnerable to Post Traumatic Stress Disorder and alcohol abuse while right brainers often are dyslexic (see Two Human Species Exist book).

Summary of Hemisity Discoveries: Surprising Significance to Daily Life

So, what have we learned so far? We have found that many of the behavioral differences between individuals are not due to sex differences. Rather, they result from hemisity differences. That is, not only do conservative left-brain men <u>but also left-brain women</u> tend to avoid feelings and keep talk to a minimum, resist listening to advice, competitively seek power and status, use a win-lose approach, are hierarchal and excusive, dress for success, don't read others minds well, thrive in chaos, are oriented toward important details, seek short-term quick solutions, are covert, and avoid responsibility for error. Their religious experience is tends to be non-emotional, legalistic and abstract, including many high church, symbolic artistic representations, and rituals.

In great contrast, not only do charismatic right-brain women but also right-brain men, tend to talk about feelings, seek advice, are cooperative, inclusive, and egalitarian, are original in dress, can read what others are thinking, are distracted by chaos, seek long term solutions, are concerned about the big picture, are transparent, cooperative, use a win-win approach and accept responsibility. In terms of religion, their experience is personal, profound, and emotional.

Judging the Hemisity of Others: Public Figures, Entertainers, and Historical Figures

Once the basic understanding of hemisity had become thoroughly internalized, I found that I could quite accurately prejudge the hemisity of others. I became so adept at this that it was rare for the later hemisity test-based determination of an individual's hemisity to be different than my pre-test estimate. To the adept, the hemisity of a person on the street, in the movies, or on TV is written all over them. Further, with biographical information, recorded statements, and photos it becomes possible to estimate the hemisity of historic figures. Based upon this approach, as may be seen in **Table 11**, each of the four hemisity subtypes are well represented among notorious composers, rulers, leaders, Nobel laureates and performers.

My most recent publication (2014) regarding 1049 high school students demonstrated that there are as many LPs with correspondingly smaller corpus callosal size, as there were RPs with a larger corpus callosal size.

Table 11: Estimates of the Hemisity of Famous People:

RMs	LMs	RFs	LFs
J.S. Bach	Claude Faure	Joan of Arc	Mother Teresa
W. A. Mozart	P.I. Tchaikovsky	Catherine the Great	Jane Goodall
Jack Kennedy	Jimmy Carter	Oprah Winfrey	Jackie Kennedy
Bill Clinton	Al Gore	Margaret Thatcher	Nancy Reagan
Francis Crick	James Watson	Marie Curie	Dorothy Hodgkin
Craig Venter	Francis Collins	Barbara McClintock	Rigoberta Menchu
Sean Connery	George Bronson	Sophia Loren	Nichole Kidman
Mel Gibson	Clint Eastwood	Salma Hayek	Sandra Bullock

So, why and how did the hemisity distributions occur so that in certain populations, LMs and RFs predominate over RMs and LFs and vice versa? Each new discovery has opened new questions and larger confrontations with traditional views.

CHAPTER 6: Historical Impact of Hemisity upon Society and Civilization

The Opposite Data-processing Orientations of the Two Cerebral Hemisphere Modules

As described above, our hemisity is determined by which side of the brain our subconscious Executive Ego is imbedded, because each hemisphere provides a unique perspective to the Executive Ego. The Executive Ego's function is to subconsciously determine which of our subcortical elements to use to produce maximal survival optimizing behavior. That is, should it assign output to our self-oriented Id or let our social brain Superego to do the job? *In fact, it has been shown that any behavioral decision and response is launched beneath consciousness almost one second before it enters our consciousness* Clearly, the hemisphere within which the Executive is embedded has the predominant influence on the Executive's behavioral orientation to produce behavioral differences of hemisity.

With this background in place, we can now begin to look at the profound differences in views of life between the divided hemispheres, which also are the source of our self-consciousness. They are separated because they each analyze data they receive in a fundamentally opposite manner.

The left hemisphere is a specialized information processing module that evolved over the eons for the top-down processing of information. It splits a whole element into its parts, then divides those parts into their subunits, and then dissects those subunits further looking for their building blocks. This top-down skill contributed to the development of language and mathematics. It moves from the general to the particular, which is the definition of deductive reasoning. It is logical. It spots differences. It sees the structures. It removes context to reveal the concept, often in 2D. It is oriented toward dissection, degradation, disintegration, and consequently destruction.

In contrast, the right hemisphere is a powerful bottom-up processor evolved to build larger structures from available building blocks, for the synthesis of new wholes, to construct things from parts. It moves from the particular to the general to produce inductive reasoning. It is empirical-experimental. It sees commonalities. It sees processes. It sees the context, often in 3D. It is the ultimate creator-builder. The combinatory synthesis of a greater whole always results in the appearance emergent properties that are often valuable. For example, the automobile with its emergent properties, locomotion and transportation, that are not possessed by its separate engine, chassis, or other parts. Or consider this: from the combination of two sticks and a string came archery.

Viewing the Two Hemispheres as Advisors, Each with a Different Point of View, Both Correct

Thousands of research reports on the contrasting properties of the right and left hemisphere have been compiled by Ian McGilchrist in his book: "The Master and His Emissary, the Divided Brain and the Making of the Western World", Yale University Press, 2009. It is the most extensive resource of specific data and their implications on this topic in existence. This chapter summarizes the book with added commentary. McGilchrist rapidly develops the view that each hemisphere acts as an independent mental module, actually as a separate mind, as was confirmed in split-brain subjects. Both evaluate how best to maximize the survival of the larger personal whole, each from their unique and valid perspectives. Thus, each cerebral hemisphere deals with words or images in a different way. They produce two different realities of the world, both of importance, each with two different ways of thinking and being. These can be complementary or competitive-conflicting. Each provides an analysis of reality that is essential for the survival of the whole person and without which that person or group will be substantially impaired.

These hemispheric modular advisors make their viewpoints known to the preconscious Executive Ego who then judges what behavioral course of action to direct. This idea is strongly supported by the split-brain studies described in Chapter 2 where two independent personalities temporarily appeared after commissurotomy. Each hemisphere has complementary but conflicting tasks. Each knows things the other does not, and needs to maintain this ignorance via corpus callosal cross inhibition and facilitation. Splitting does not cause a deficit, but an excess. Split brainers ultimately are not handicapped because both hemispheres learn first to forward their information to the subcortical Executive Ego who directs the behavioral outcome. It has been shown by Benjamin

Libet and others that a subconscious executive element decides and initiates behavior between about 0.5 to an incredible 7 seconds before we become conscious of its choice. The executive, which is privy to inputs from both hemispheres, somehow adapts to their conflicting points of view to produce a unified behavior.

A partial list of what each of the hemispheres has been found to do can be seen in **Table 12.** The modern neuroscience techniques that have been used to obtain these data include the assessment of unilateral stroke patients, unilateral hemisphere incapacitation by the Wada Test, unilateral transmagnetic stimulation (TMS), electrocortical stimulation (ECS), electroconvulsive therapy (ECT), tachistoscopy, dichotic listening, split brains studies, electro encephalography EEG, magnetic resonance imaging (MRI), functional magnetic resonance imaging (fMRI), single photo emission computed tomography (SPECT), and positron emission tomography (PET).

Brain Wiring Differences

I have written out the contents of **Table 12** in prose here. Thus, in terms of brain wiring differences, the left cerebral hemisphere (LH) sees only the right foreground and often denies the existence of left appendages. In contrast the right hemisphere (RH) sees the left foreground and both backgrounds. Split brainers cannot identify objects with their right hand (a LH deficit), but can with their left hand (a RH skill). The LH has local wiring

Table 12: What the Two Hemispheres Can and Cannot Do

Left Hemisphere	Right Hemisphere
WIRING DIFFERENCES	
Sees only right foreground, denies left appendages	Sees left foreground, both sides background
Split brainers can't identify things with the R hand	Split brainers identify things with the L hand
Local wiring, fewer cross region connections	Global wiring, regions widely interconnected
Cannot use tools or follow a sequence or a recipe	Can use tools, can make a cup of coffee
Cannot follow a narrative, cannot read minds	Enjoys stories, reads minds, source of ideas
Parasympathetic control of the familiar	Sympathetic control for dealing with the new
Looks at other's mouth (detects anger, not deceit)	Looks at other's eyes (sees emotions, deceit)
ANALYTICAL DIFFERENCES	
Top-down, details, divides, sees parts	Bottom-up, overview, integrates, sees whole
Sees trees, content, removes context as irrelevant	Sees forest and context as unique, important
Abstracts, distinguishes, 2D, deduction	Combines, synthesizes, 3D, induction
Language, mathematics, binary	Spatial: faces, facial emotions, analogue
Divided attention, selectivity, discriminates	Focused attention, intensity, synthesizes
Considers structures, the what of things	Considers activities, the how of things
Makes rules, categories, divisions, distinctions	Deals with whole experience, randomness
Denies discrepancies, rigid, unrealistic	Alert for change, flexible, creative, realistic
Re-presents with symbols, literal, knows	Uses original context, metaphor, understand
Stays within the data, likes rationality	Extrapolates beyond the data, prefers reason
Categorizes present information	Explores, gathers new information
Makes tools, machines, speech, melody	Uses tools, processes, creates music harmony
EMOTIONALITY	
LH music is not emotional	RH music is emotional, sad, subcortical
Autistic, doesn't understand others, depersonalizes	Self-aware, understands others, has empathy
Lives in virtual world of its own creation	In touch with the reality and with Superego
Cheerful after a RH stroke, mania	Depressed after a LH stroke, depression
Must win, be right, would rather die than lose	Would rather lose, but be alive
SOCIAL ORIENTATION	
Malicious, confabulates, lies, no concern for others	Compassionate, tells the truth, empathetic
Has a Reporter-Interpreter personality	Has an Imaginer-Visualizer personality
Favors self, seeks selfish gain, impersonal, autistic	Altruistic, favors, group, family, personal
Likes the traditional, predictability	Is innovative, seeks new possibilities
Schizophrenic, sees others as nonliving imposters	Sees life, aliveness in others
Views the body as an object	Sees the body as alive
Lacks sense of past or future	Understands history
Shows religious legalism	Has personal experience of spirituality

with few cross region connections; the RH has global wiring with many regions interconnected. The LH cannot use tools, or follow recipe sequences. The RH can use tools and make a cup of coffee. The LH cannot follow a narrative or read minds, while the RH enjoys stories, reads minds, and is a source of ideas. The LH uses para-sympathetic control of the familiar, while the RH deals with new data with the sympathetic system. The LH looks others in the mouth to detect anger or deceit. The RH looks at the eyes to detect emotions but not deceit.

Analytical Differences

In terms of analytical differences, the LH is top-down oriented, seeing details and dividing things into parts, while the RH is bottom-up oriented, seeing the overview and integrating it to see the whole. The LH sees the trees and content, removing the context as irrelevant; the RH sees the forest and holds the context as unique and important. The LH abstracts and distinguishes things into 2 dimensions by deduction. The RH combines and synthesizes 3 dimensions by induction. The binary LH was the source of language and mathematics, The ana-logue RH is spatial, recognizing faces and their emotions. The LH provides divided attention, selectivity, and dis-crimination. The RH provides intense focused attention and synthesizes options. The LH looks at structures: the what of things. The RH considers activities: the how of things. The LH make distinctions, divisions, categories, and rules. The RH deals with the whole experience, including randomness. The LH is rigid, unrealistic, and denies discrepancies. The RH is alert for change, flexible, realistic, and creative. The LH re-presents things with symbols, is literal and knows. The RH uses the original context to understand and then to create metaphors. The LH stays within the data and likes rationality. The RH extrapolates beyond the data and prefers reason. The LH categorizes present information, while the RH explores and gathers new information. The LH makes tools and machines, speech and melody. The RH uses tools and processes, and creates musical harmony.

Emotionality

As regards to emotionality, LH music is not emotional, while RH music often is sad and subcortical. The LH is autistic and doesn't understand others, it depersonalizes them. The RH is self-aware, empathetic, and understands others. The LH lives in a virtual world, while the RH is in touch with reality and also with the Superego. The LH is cheerfully manic after a RH stroke. The RH is depressed after a LH stroke. The LH must win, be right, and would rather die than lose. The RH would rather lose and stay alive.

Social Orientation

Regarding social orientation, the LH is malicious, and lies with no concern for others. The RH is compassionate, empathetic, and tells the truth. The LH personality is like a Reporter-Interpreter, saying what happened. The RH is an Imaginative-Visualizer type personality that sees what happened. The LH is impersonal and seeks selfish gain. The RH is personal, altruistic, and favors the family group. The LH likes the traditional and predictability. The RH is innovative and seeks new possibilities. The LH is schizophrenic seeing others as nonliving imposters. The RH sees aliveness in others. The LH views the body as an object, while the RH sees the body as alive. The LH lacks a sense of past or future. The RH understands history. The LH shows religious legalism, while the RH has a personal experience of spirituality.

McGilchrist, provides published evidence that the RH is a source of imagination, creativity, religious awe, music, dance, poetry, art, love of nature, moral sense, humor, non-verbal communication, and ability to change one's mind. In contrast, the LH has contributed the language systems upon which civilization has been built. He goes farther to propose that each of the hemispheres can be viewed as a separate entity with characteristic attitudes and personality traits. In his book, he develops this theme, of naming facts, rationality, mapping, fixity, abstraction, generalities, categorization, control, precision, rules, and extensively, providing strong supporting evidence for these characterizations from the primary neuroscience literature. A compilation of these personality traits is presented in **Table 13**. Fortunately, these contrasts are self-evident and will not be individually supported here, a job extensively done by McGilchrist in

Table 13: The Hemispheres as Separate Entities, According to McGilchrist

Left Hemisphere	Right Hemisphere
PERSONALITIES	
impersonal, distancing, avoidant	personal, direct, gazes into face
a predator, alienated from others	concerned and caring for others
likes knowledge, certainty	truth as a proposal, a possibility, a belief
uses its will to control others	uses its will to care for others
rejects what is, acts to change things	chooses, accepts what is as perfect
disembodied, unfeeling, utilitarian	alive, emotional sees beauty, appreciates
overconfident, lacks insight of the big picture	humble, understands the overview
will lie to cover ignorance or to control	is honest, creates trust and cooperation
seeks power, mechanical, dissects, abstracts	passionate, humorous, intuitive, religious
alienated, has lost meaning, dead	animated, joy of meaning, alive
thinking, explicit, rational	feeling, implicit, intuitive
agrees with false premise, because said to be true	thinks false premises/conclusions are absurd
gullible, accepts the absurd	bullshit detector, Devil's advocate
APPROACHES	
pins things down, clear, precise, analytical	philosophizes, sees Godel's incompleteness
rational, its ideas appear to it to be the truth	paradox: part vs. whole, river flow: same/dif
divides into smaller and smaller dead parts	unites into larger living wholes, alive
dissection, dissociation, destructive, deadly	synthesis, creation, assembly, emergence
static, unchanging, precise, explicit	contrasting, relative, approximation, implicit
abstract, abbreviated, symbolic	whole, visual, seeing is knowing
familiar, "re-presented", expected	presented anew, unexpected
cannot know new things	creative, an idea, unique, wonder, unveiling
speech, logic, linearity, analytical, sequential	thought, parallel, network
flat, 2D, contextless, plane of focus	deep, 3D, contextual, outside of focus
ATTITUDES	
views world as series of static, finished entities	views world as a process, always in flux
won't take responsibility, blames others	responsible, blames self
believes it is in control, the originator	knows the Other (Superego) exists
is either omnipotent or impotent, either I or not I	there is something Other that we can reach
believes authorities	believes own senses
utility, selfish gain	empathy, altruism, gain for the group
dull, conceptualized, inauthentic, thru a window	lived experience, real, direct
reductive, descriptive clarity, loss of wonder	awe from the larger context
values serve its own pleasure	values serve the holy
the arrival	the journey, evolving process, progress
a what-ness, self as a thing	a how-ness, self is a process.
accepts the known as the truth	approximates truth, seeks a better metaphor
"I think, therefore I am."	"I feel, therefore I am".
sees the universe is a mass of things	longs for something above the universe
would rather deny paralyzed limb than be wrong	does not deny, may become depressed
will repeat error hoping for success next time	knows when to change tactics

---

PROPERTIES

The Emissary	more closely connected to the true Master
views light as a particle	views light as a wave
oriented toward explanation, clarity	oriented toward wonder, awe
focused attention, division, abstract, explicit	broad vigilant attention of whole, implicit
conflates episodes out of sequence	remembers the first presentation of episodes
meaning is lost, alienation, cannot extrapolate	source of meaning, projects beyond data
linear, local, division, disintegrates	parallel and distributed, unification, builds
conformist, zombie, dissociated, spectator	original, alive, connected, participant
fragmented, amnestic, unfeeling, hypnotized	intact, feeling, clear, awake

his book. Although a table is a compact way of compiling facts, I have written them out here in prose as well.

Personalities

Thus, according to McGilchrist, regarding personality differences between the cerebral hemispheres, the LH tends to be impersonal, distant, and avoidant, while the RH is personal, direct, and gazes into one's face. The LH is a predator, alienated from others, while the RH is concerned about and caring of others. The LH likes knowledge and certainty. For the RH, truth is a proposal, a possibility, a belief. The LH uses its will to control others. The RH uses its will to care for others. The LH rejects what is and acts to change things, while the RH chooses what is as perfect. The LH is disembodied, unfeeling, and utilitarian. The RH is alive, emotional and sees and appreciates beauty. The LH is overconfident and lacks insight of the big picture; the RH is humble and understands the overview. The LH acts to cover its ignorance or to control. The RH is honest and creates trust and cooperation. The LH seeks power and is mechanical, dissecting and abstracting. The RH is passionate, humorous, intuitive, and religious. The LH is alienated, has lost its meaning, and is dead. The RH is animated with the joy of meaning and is alive. The LH is thinking, explicit, and rational; the RH is feeling, implicit, and intuitive. The LH agrees with a false premise because someone said it was true. The RH thinks conclusions based upon a false premise to be absurd. The LH is gullible and accepts the absurd. The RH is a bullshit detector and a Devil's advocate.

Approaches

The two hemispheres have very different approaches. The LH pins things down, is clear, precise, and analytical. The RH philosophizes, sees Godel's incompleteness of systems. The LH is rational; its ideas appear to it to be the truth. The RH recognizes the paradoxicality of the parts vs. the whole, and the flow of a river, the same yet always different. The LH divides into smaller and smaller ultimately dead parts, The RH unites parts into larger living wholes. The LH dissects, dissociates, and destroys. The RH synthesizes, creates, assembles, and emerges alive. The LH is static, unchanging, precise, and explicit. The RH is contrasting, relative, and an implicit approximation. The LH is abstract, abbreviated, and symbolic. The RH is visual where seeing the whole is knowing. The LH "re-presents" the expected and familiar. It cannot know new things. The RH presents the world anew as an unveiling of an unexpected wonderful new idea. The LH is logical, analytical, and sequential. The RH recognizes parallel network possibilities. The world of the LH is flat, two dimensional, only in the plane of focus. The world of the RH is deep, three dimensional, contextual, beyond just the plane of focus.

Attitudes

In terms of differences in attitudes, the LH views the world as a series of static finished entities, while the RH views the world as a process, always in flux. The LH won't take responsibility, but rather blames others. The RH is responsible and often blames itself. The LH believes it is in control and the originator of actions, while the RH knows the subconscious Superego exists. The LH is either omnipotent or impotent, either I or not I. The RH knows that there is a subconscious Source that we can reach. The LH believes authorities, while the RH believes its own senses. The LH seeks utility and selfish gain; the RH promotes empathy and altruistic gain for the group. The LH reduces things to dull inauthentic concepts as through a window, the RH lives real and direct experience. The LH by reducing things to their descriptive clarity causes a loss of wonder. The RH is in awe of the larger context. LH values serve its own pleasure; RH values serve the holy. The LH lives for the arrival, while the RH enjoys the progress of the journey with its evolving process. The LH views the whatness of the self as a thing; The RH views the howness of the self as process. The LH accepts what is known as the truth; The RH approximates the truth while seeking a better metaphor. The LH sees the universe as a mass of things. The RH longs for something beyond the universe. The LH would rather deny a paralyzed limb than be wrong. The RH will not deny, but may become depressed. The LH will endlessly repeat an error hoping for success the next time. The RH knows when to change tactics.

Properties

Regarding the differences in properties, The LH is the Emissary; the RH is more closely connected to the true Master. The LH views light as a particle; the RH views light as a wave. The LH is oriented toward explanatory clarity; the RH is oriented toward wonder and awe. The LH attention is focused on the explicit abstract subdivision; the RH gives broad vigilant attention to the implicit whole. The LH conflates and distorts episodes out of sequence; the RH remembers the first presentation of episodes. The LH loses meaning, becomes alienated, and cannot extrapolate. The RH is the source of meaning and can project beyond data to predict. The linear LH disintegrates things because its divides the local; the RH unifies and builds things because its view is parallel and distributed. The LH is a conformist dissociated zombie spectator; the RH is an original alive and connected participant. The fragmented LH is amnestic, unfeeling, and hypnotized; The intact RH is awake and clear.

Although we tend to identify with our LH or RH self-consciousness, the essential core of our being is actually subcortical. It is said that only about 5-10% of brain activity is self-conscious. "Yes, Johnny, it is true that we only use 10% of our brain. The other 90% uses us". We make decisions, solve problems, make judgments, discriminate, and reason without the need for self-conscious involvement. As repeatedly mentioned, it has been found that our Executive Ego makes decisions about one second before we become consciously aware of them. Further, the origin of our feelings and of our will is outside of self-consciousness. In fact, Decartes' "I think, therefore I am", is less accurate than "I feel, therefore I am". The RH has been shown to be more closely connected with our unconscious cerebellar social brain Superego than the LH. Thus, it tends to be the more emotional hemisphere.

Contributions of the Two Hemispheric Advisors to the Development of Western Civilization

McGilchrist has taken his analysis two steps farther. First, he has given the RH consciousness element executive-like properties, calling it the "Master", and has viewed the skillful LH as the valued assistant of the RH, calling it the "Emissary". Second, he then provides compelling evidence that the somewhat antisocial LH value system of the Emissary has slowly overcome the more pro social values of the RH Master, so that in the recent centuries society has become increasingly decadent and sterile.

When McGilchrist wrote "The Master and his Emissary", he was unaware of hemisity and had discarded the idea of hemisphericity. He gave no direct mechanism to describe how LH or RH values could be promulgated into culture or could oscillate in public favor over time. Yet, as we will see, tracing the history of humanity indeed shows the footprints of both the Master and his Emissary over time.

It is tempting to speculate how the RH and LH by way of hemisity may have contributed to the building of civilization. It is now known that in an unsorted population there are nearly equal numbers of males and females, and more importantly here, that there are equal numbers of right brain-oriented persons (RPs) and LPs. The question is: how could this constancy cause surges of right-brain thought alternating with left-brain thought in subsequent cultures? Recently, we have reported that considerable hemisity sorting occurs within the professions. Thus as might be expected, astronomers, engineers and architects dealing with the big picture were found to be enriched in RPs and while particle physicists, accountants and librarians focusing upon important details were enriched in LPs. Further, it is a strategically important fact that until very recently only males have occupied the top ranks in essentially all professions.

Thus, it would appear that over history, with notable exceptions, only right and left brain-oriented males (RMs and LMs) have shaped public fashion and popular thought. Public thought is a gossip and dominance-based, shifting community consensus of ideas that strongly influence individual thinking. Since the invention of writing, consensus thinking leading to the accumulation of respected literature has shaped the accepted values of public opinion. This public thinking of the community leaders, that is, of the RM or LM leaders, tended to influence all secondary decisions, derivative ideas, and beliefs. The idea of the existence of ancient population bands of opposite hemisity across the eastern hemisphere will be developed later in this book.

At first, it was the patriarch and his clansmen, then the village chief and his henchmen that shaped the culture of the village. Later, warriors were replaced by the specialists: hunters, ranchers, tool makers, artisans. These were again replaced by the King, his knights, philosophers, mathematicians, scholars, and priests. The hemisity of the king, had a great bearing in his actions and choices of advisors and their behavior. Thus different nations followed the crooked course of history, often influenced by the hemisity of their leader and his court. Similarly, in philosophy, music, and art, the hemisity of the trend setters resulted in the development of different RH- or LH-oriented traditions.

Hemisity provides a powerful new perspective for the understanding of history. A cause and effect analysis of the effect of hemisity upon history has now become possible and will no doubt be developed extensively, thus rewriting the details of history in a most fascinating manner. Yet this is not necessary for our purposes here. It is sufficient to follow McGilchrist's outlines in brief below of the effect of the Master and his Emissary upon the stages of the development of Western Civilization to be convinced of the importance their conflicts upon history.

Contributions of the Greeks: 800-340 BC

The following major elements of civilization were produced by the Greeks: the production of objective knowledge, a constitution, a body of laws, philosophy, study of history, geography, an educational system, types of architecture, the study of anatomy, zoology, medicine, geometry, physics, logic, mathematics, moral and political philosophy, truth as knowable and consistent, ideas, forms, categories, abstractions, the first known democracy, the first Olympic games, classical art and sculpture, mythology as religion, the idea of an immortal soul, drama, comedy, tragedy, epic poetry, and massive theaters. This was an explosion of intelligence and wisdom such as the world had never seen!

The right hemispheric orientation was toward the wonder of existence, poetry, music, drama, sculpture, architecture, empathy, humor, sense of self, knowing one's self, and the Eleusinian mysteries. However, the left hemisphere increasingly saw the world as a deception, where thought is all there is. If couldn't be thought, it could not exist. This resulted in a world of ideals, fixed beliefs, a realm of forms, and universal abstractions. Actual things were seen by the LH as inferior to true realities, where the absolute and eternal were knowable by only by logic. The LH distrusted intuition, the implicit, and common sense. This lead to a degeneration to the absurdly rational. Plato asserted that the soul was a transmigrated prisoner of the body. In Plato's world, music was outlawed except for utilitarian purposes.

Contributions of the Romans: 100 BC-AD 300

According to McGilchrist, most of the Roman legacy was contributed during the 50 years of the Augustan era of the 1st century BC. Major RH advances were the development of arches in aqueducts and viaducts, highways, invention of concrete, architecture using the dome, and the construction of coliseums and their use in mass entertainment. The Roman alphabet was invented, the Roman legal system jurisprudence was established. There was an increase in psychological sophistication, including the ideal of reasonableness, a further understanding of nature, of human bonds, and a sense of pity.

The LH contributed important developments including the codification of law, solidarity, and administrative rigidity. But, this was accompanied by a loss of flexibility, imagination, and originality. There followed increasing standardization, equalization, uniformity, homogeneity, with a centralized hierarchy of civil officials and global coordination. Truth was to be proved by argument, where rationality triumphs. Money, utility, and profit replace gifts, reciprocity, and relationships. There was a loss of a sense of the whole and of the individual. Authoritarian laws and prohibitions multiplied, along for a passion for control, fixity, uniformity, abstraction, and suppression of independent thought. Constantine nationalized Christianity. Rome fell due to over-taxation and underfunding of the army. Civil war broke out, barbarism overran the country, and civilization collapsed,

Contributions of Christianity and the Dark Ages: AD 500-1200.

Under the Roman Catholic Church, it appears that no advances were made in math, science, culture, politics, or religion for many centuries. Civilization slowly atrophied.

Contributions of the Renaissance: AD 1400-1700

After a thousand years of stasis, a great thirst for knowledge of the natural world emerged. This led to the beginnings of modern science, history, philosophy, and arts. There was a great resurgence of the influence of the RH, even beyond that in the ancient world. Humanity climbed a hill and saw what was always there for all to see but none before had seen. Perspective was restored by a return to looking at things as they are, not as a Greek ideal or what was thought to be known. Perspective in art was also restored. It had been lost for over 1000 years, until Giotto's work in the 14th century. RH emotionality returned. Shakespeare emerged with his complete disregard of theory and category. Rather, his was a celebration of the richness of human variety. The Renaissance fostered the greatest output of religious art in history. The Renaissance man integrated the disciplines. Joy appeared but was melancholy, as in requiems with sadness and fear. Yearning was at the heart of Renaissance music and art, a longing for a reunion with the spiritual.

Contributions of the Reformation: AD 1517-1648

In the Reformation, religious hatreds rapidly developed based upon "either/or" considerations. Was this the truth or a falsehood? Was this God or an idol? Was the truth literal or metaphorical? A LH rejection of the RH's growing exuberance occurred in a renewed attempt to find certainty. All mystery was prohibited so as to regain "authenticity". There was a triumph of written word, idolized, enduring, and changeless. Protestantism developed, along with capitalism and bureaucratization. There became an overriding interest in self-protection, self-assertion, self-expansion. Experts were specialists. Free thinking was used to throw off tyranny, superstition, and wrong. An individual will to power became strongly anti-traditional, leading to the removal of holy places and the replacement of the religious with a secular power structure. Sin was punished, and hierarchal classes were produced. Income was sought in the form of psychologically coerced offerings. There was an attack on music, on past wisdom, on context. The previously sacred was violently desecrated. The magical transubstantiation metaphor "hoc est enim corpus meum: for this is my body" became "Hocus pocus". The original RH Protestant rebellion against empty corrupt Catholic practices became over-taken by the LH so as to produce the same situation in the Protestant churches.

Contributions of the Enlightenment: Late AD 1700-1800s

This was a period of the highest achievement yet seen, marked by harmony and balance. The world had become clear, orderly, fixed, certain, knowable. The three foundations of the Enlightenment, which were known since Plato, now became the public viewpoint:

1. All genuine questions can be answered. If not, it is not a question.
2. All answers are knowable. They can be discovered by means that can be taught to others.
3. All answers must be compatible and non-contradictory with one another.

The world became single, knowable, consistent, certain, fixed, finite, generalizable, a closed system that could be mastered. For clarity, this view focused upon commonalities, avoided individual differences and the contingencies of the outside beyond. Capitalism was the child of Enlightenment. It developed rules for human conduct, then codified and internationalized them. It emphasized the maximization of profit.

Two major transformations in society occurred with contrasting extremes. The French Revolution, where as much as possible was done to bring about freedom, and the American Revolution where as little as possible was done, placing as few restraints as possible to maintain freedom. Haydn and Mozart were products of the enlightenment in art.

Mathematical symmetry was developed: do the same to both sides of the equation to find the absolute, but not a real world solution. The LH through surveillance sought a deceptive utilitarian clarity. However its goals of liberty, equality, fraternity could only be obtained by the RH. The LH was rational but not reasonable.

Rene Descartes, an influential philosopher from the 1600s who had a profound impact on this period, exemplified extreme LH thinking. He believed that body senses and imagination were the source of error and a schizophrenia-like madness. Actually his ideas themselves seem schizophrenic. They were excessively attached to LH hyper-rationality and were reflexively self-aware, disembodied, and alienated. He wished to be detached from hunger and pain. He felt he could only infer that his body exists, and he doubted the existence of other persons, other than as dressed up machines. He wished to be detached from his body, emotions, mortality. He wished to be a spectator, not an actor of the world's comedies. His was the world of representation, of certainty, fixity, objectification control, and emotional non-engagement, empty of all meaning and mechanical. Boredom was his passive view of existence, the endless present. One of his fallacies has derailed western thinking for three centuries. It was "Things that we can conceive very clearly and distinctly are all true". Thus, the dualistic immortal soul existed for him.

Enlightenment's LH dark side was to monitor, control, constrict, and repress in search of power. Phantasmagoria, the grotesque, hallucinatory reveries, paranoia, and nightmarish fantasy emerged. Mechanical descriptions of life appeared, such as "a marriage is an agreement for the reciprocal use of each other's sex organs", or "laughter was a sound produced by a mechanical billows", all indicating a diminished RH presence.

Contributions of Romanticism: AD 1800-1850

The Romantic Revolution was the RH backlash to the Age of Enlightenment. The idea of individual differences was central here, where differences are seen to be as important as generalities. A thing and its opposite could both be true, as illustrated in the famous "thesis, antithesis, and synthesis". Reason was seen as insufficient and incomplete, where theory was felt to be incompatible with experience. There was a recursion to the Renaissance, accompanied by a rediscovery of Shakespeare. As opposed to the Enlightenment, the fusion of body, mind, and soul or spirit was keenly felt by the Romantics, such as William Blake. Longing for personal and historical past was a central theme of Romanticism. The concept of the sublime expands and extends the beholder toward a sense of belonging to something greater than oneself, toward the lost Other with profundity, reverence and depth. Romanticism called forth the RH world.

Contributions of the Industrial Revolution: AD 1760-1840

In the Industrial Revolution, LH materialism and positivism emerge. From that view, ideals and ideas such as God, were felt to keep us in a state of indignity and humiliating superstition. They instead took an either/or, literal, "Science is the only way" interpretation, mistrusting imagination, and ignoring context. Reality and authenticity was said to be based upon what you can touch with your hands. During this time, the denial of the divine was as important as was the elevation of the material. The divine was replaced by scientific materialism. Dialectical materialism opposed groundless authority. Science was held to be the only authority.

The LH's lack of concern for context led to the application of scientism to the human condition in a manner that was completely out of context. Claims of exemption from historical criticism produced a sense of infallibility and led to assertions that the scientific method was the only valid way to find answers to human problems. This led to the Industrial Revolution which applied scientific materialism to produce lifeless machines making other lifeless machines to make typical invariant lifeless forms. This ultimately created unnatural, managed urban environments where most humans now live in isolation in a virtual life of work, TV, and the internet. That is, a world of the LH with no escape to the RH world and to ancient spirituality.

Contributions of Modernism: AD 1920-

According to McGilchrist, by around 1920 human character appeared to change so that all human relations shifted, i.e., between masters-servants, husbands-wives, parents-children, religion, the conduct of politics and literature. A social disintegration resulted, caused by many elements, including industrial expansion, an altered view of the individual, the drift from rural to urban, the breakdown of social orders, a loss of belonging, an expanded mental life, and scientific materialism producing a disenchanted world, leading to capitalism, consumerism, and relationships based upon utility. Greed and competition eliminated the former felt connections and cultural continuity. The state emerged as organizing, categorizing, and subjugating all into conformity. An adulation of power seeking and of material force led to the abandonment of socialism and the rise of totalitarianism. Abstraction, bureaucratization and social dislocation now left life with no meaning. Capitalism caused globalization which destroyed belonging and meaning, and created homelessness. The LH became increasingly antagonistic to RH values. Problems arose due to mobility, a rapid change of the environment, and fragmentation of social bonds in communities, producing loss of place and personal isolation.

The LH triumph produced a kind of schizophrenia: i.e., the inability to take another's point of view (loss of theory of mind), and the inability to see the big picture. This was accompanied by a loss of intuition and the ability to understand metaphor, loss of the ability to follow narrative and the flow of time, a process. The LH sees only points in time. The LH began to show a loss of reality and common sense. It instead intellectualized, schematized, made rules of utility, machine-like with its tools. Seeing only details alienated it from the context of existence, disturbed its relationship with self and the world, to become hyper self-conscious. Its loss of automaticity and reflexes required it to plan of every move. LH schizophrenia, due to its instability of context, becomes a hall of mirrors. Its loss of feeling and loss of self as actor led it to the passivity of a spectator. A loss of the context of life and of survival led it to a clinical detachment from life, like a corpse.

Now, according to McGilchrist, experience no longer had value. Over explicit consciousness caused depersonalization and alienation from the body at a social level. Derealization, unworlding devoid of human significance, the Ego became a passive voyeur. There was no true world, just one of our own creation, by a skeptical, self-referencing consciousness which watches itself. There was a loss of meaning. The interpreter is not the originator, but a facilitator interpreting itself, lonely, isolated from RH and the Other. Its task is to look for meaning. But without the RH, it has no anchor in reality. It becomes paranoid, confused, everything-nothing, omnipotent-impotent. Empty restless boredom leads to sensationalism in advertising and entertainment, seeking novelty and shock value. It is sad because it can find only what it already knows. It lacks newness of imagination. LH becomes obsessed with structures, with the "organization man", bureaucracy, communism, capitalism, socialism. Materialist abstractions and concepts become things. Things become concepts, status, property, utility. Re-presentation of a thing distances us from it, substitutes an abstraction and objectifies it. The LH must make rules to bring it under control. Reality disintegrates into a map, the LH Interpreter becomes its own God.

Boredom causes passivity, indifference, loneliness, fear, anxiety. It becomes schizophrenic due to the RH deficit. Actual schizophrenia as an illness became common with industrial development, with moving from the rural, and with increases in population density. It was accompanied with the appearance of anorexia, cutting, burning, multiple personality disorder (MPD), dissociation, bipolar personality disorder (BPD), autism, and Asperger's Syndrome. Guilt is rampant. The isolated LH tends toward autism: inability to tell what another is thinking, lack of social intelligence, difficulty in nonverbal communication, lack of emotional tone, humor, or irony, the inability to detect deceit, difficulty with implications, lack of empathy, of imagination, attraction to the mechanical. Autism treats people and body parts as inanimate objects, manifests alienation from or lack of self, shows lack of contact and obsession with detail. Social isolation led to exaggerated fear, violence, and aggression, thus further isolation. LH dominated persons are found to be suitable for employment in science, technology, and administration, which now shapes the world.

Modern art, such as Absurdism and Dadaism emerged--- focused on structure over the process beyond.

Alienated, fragmented, and decontexualized, it cut off of all roots of meaning, shared value or experiences. It is dead. It thrives on novel fusion of known objects in unnatural and menacing ways. Nazis and Stalinists were against originality and imagination in art, but were pro novelty and banality. Modern art becomes geometric shapes, with no faces. Abstract art and cinema come from modernism. It is ironic that RH music with melody, harmony and rhythm is the most compelling of the arts and is needed for mental health, with its conflict and resolution, discord leading to harmony. Pathetically, the LH has abstracted music down just to rhythm. Jazz is a creation of modernism, which could not abandon music completely.

Contributions of the Post Modernism

In McGilchrist's view, post modernism drains all meaning into codes in a psychopathic manner: for example, in scientific postmodernism indeterminancy, which affirms there is no reality or truth to determine or interpret, only the ecstasy of chaos. The omnipotence and impotence of schizophrenia is present in art critics. Reductionism makes people feel powerful by explaining away the mysterious. Psychoanalysts and scientists are tempted to use their position to manipulate the innocent as a form of power. Science, the philosophy of our age, corrodes higher values and causes cynicism, and materialism. Now ongoing in the debate on nature of consciousness, the skeptics are smug and superior. Conversely, neuroscientists pretend to understand it, thus making the rest of us ignorant.

The Master betrayed

Finally, McGilchrist outlines the present extreme imbalance of the talented LH "Emissary" over his RH "Master". For example, the essential elements of bureaucracy include the necessity of procedures that are known, organizability, predictability, a concept of justice where the individual is reduced to a mere quality, and an explicit abstraction. The personal is reified toward the mechanical: 1 how much can it do? 2. How fast? 3. How precise? There is a loss of context so that a person becomes annihilated into an identical unit, a number on a production line, an object. The world is fragmented into random disconnected pieces, organized for maximum utility. No higher human values remain, only cynicism and selfishness. Material things replace the living. Relationships are depersonalized, leading to exploitation, rather than cooperation with persons or the world. Uniformity of race and sex lead to resentment and paranoia at all levels. Totalitarianism follows with loss of liberty, monitoring, loss of privacy, and increase in power of the state. Personal responsibility decreases. The LH sees altruism as a threat to its self-interest. It must be in control, but without responsibility to others. Afraid of death and obsessed with explicit sex, the omnipresent LH loses common sense insight. Professionals are distrusted and brought under control. Loss of meaning leads to craving for novelty and stimulation. Flow becomes pieces, loss of uniqueness, replacement by theory, a rise in explicitness, loss of intuitive moral sense. People become spectators, not actors. Arts are degraded. The body becomes a machine, addressed with technical specific language.

All this is justified by the LH as a maximization of happiness. But actually a loss of satisfaction and enjoyment of work, a loss of happiness has occurred instead. What brings happiness? Not health, not wealth. There has been an increase in material prosperity in Orient, US, Europe, but not happiness. Instead a hedonic treadmill ensures a permanent state of unfulfilled desire. If one rises above a minimum requirement for calories, and is provided minimum security, further increases in wealth does not bring happiness. What brings happiness is the breadth and depth of one's RH social connections. Large variations in depressive illness are linked to the degree of stability and interconnectedness within a culture. Mexican culture is much superior to US culture in terms of rates of depression. In the US since WWII, depression has doubled. Social connectedness predicts better health. Loss of close folkways and empathetic attention lead to a decline in health.

The RH needs the LH. However, although the LH contributes much to mankind as a more evolved valuable servant, it is a poor master. The LH also needs the RH, and its religion, enlightenment. LH Modernism and Postmodernism have undermined us by destroying tradition and culture, intuition, communal wisdom, common sense. History and past are gone. There is no nature in the city. Our exit from the LH hall of mirrors is blocked by the 1. Degradation of the body to a mechanism, a thing, 2. Reduction of the soul to an artifact, mocking, discounting, and dismantling it, and 3. Loss of art, which is essential for body and soul. The body should be transparent in the process of doing life. Not part of a machine. Boredom leads to pornography. The soul should be above the body. Stalinists and Puritans converted cathedrals into a urinals. LH has sacrificed the Superego Other for nothingness.

We need to recognize the existence of the Superego Other as the true master beyond the RH, seeking to optimize the survival of life. Music can restore lost soul and body. Beauty and goodness are transcendental, but now minimized from art, where skill is deemphasized. Art has been brought down from great achievement to a mere competition. At first attacks were upon the holy, now they are upon beauty. What is needed for happiness is beauty and love for the Other, not desire and pornography. Art is now used to announce wealth and status. Now nothing is holy, art has become a photo of an unmade bed, or a painting of a pile of garbage. Art should be a vehicle for body and spirit, and love for the Other. This, the LH cannot understand and sees as blocking its authority.

Part of reality is ever the same (LH), part of it is ever changing (RH). Viewing a natural environment has a healing effect. Science needs to move away from materialism. The LH foreman has rebelled against his owner upon whom he depends, and thus has created war and suffering. Our brains reflect the structure of the universe. Bottom-up, higher levels are of the RH, top-down, lower levels are the LH's domain. We need both. LH and RH have separate functions, opposed yet complementary. The divided nature of reality has been observed since the appearance of self-consciousness. It is a recurring theme through history. Two souls are divided within my breast. Understanding the incompatible top-down and bottom-up nature of the two cerebral hemispheres helps to clarify their differences in viewpoints and function.

Thus, McGilchrist in his painting of the opposite natures of the two hemispheres and of their past historic paths has led us to the present situation. However, as we shall see, there is also hope that they can discover, not that they are opposite enemies, but rather that they can be complementary friends, each contributing to a more complete understanding of reality, the universe, life, and mind.

CHAPTER 7: Knowing You Own Hemisity and That of Others can Transform Your Life

How Hemisity Resolves Motivation and Identity Conflicts Within Oneself

The common perspective that "All men are created equal" or that "All men are equal in the eyes of God" has long been a source of conflict at numerous levels. For example, on the intrapersonal level, my friend John says he hasn't remembered a dream in years, in fact, he says he doubts that he even dreams at all. He also says his thoughts of specific things consist of words, never pictures. In contrast, I often remember my dreams in detail, and when I think, I usually see things visually. Now, if I had a poor self-image, I would feel somehow inferior and defective in comparison to John. However, since I think quite well of myself, I think he is the deficient one. Of course, I would be wrong in both cases.

As any glance at the *Guinness Book of Records* will confirm, we are by no means created equal. This applies to hemisity as well. We are born either with our Executive Ego on the right or left side of our brains. This makes some of us different from certain others. That is, we fall into to two equally valid camps of perfectly normal human beings. And as such, we can "claim certain unalienable rights, among these are life, liberty, and the pursuit of happiness", unless we are criminals. Thus, neither John nor I are defective nor inferior, just biologically different. He is a LM and I a RM. We can enjoy and feel proud of our differences while accepting and appreciating the qualities of the other that we do not have.

My friend Mike loves to cook. He regales his family and friends with great meals and dinner parties. He dominates the kitchen and personally oversees every detail with gusto. His lucky wife can only be pleased. I know several men like Mike. However, I find myself interested in other things than meal preparation. Fortunately, my wife loves to cook. Why don't I care to cook? It's not that I am incapable of culinary activities. In college, I was employed for several years in a bakery and was given several raises for my work. I'm just not attracted to cooking. Yet at times I can feel jealous, inadequate, and inferior to Mike, especially when my wife and I are guests at one of his banquets. What a winner he is! Now that I have come to understand hemisity, I know that many LMs are similarly motivated as Mike, while most RMs are oriented in other directions, such as hunting and bringing in the game for others to cook. Thus, I have come to be at peace with myself while admiring Mike's culinary skills.

How Hemisity Resolves Conflicts in One's Spiritual Life

At the intrapersonal level, a potential for conflict particularly applies to one's sense of religiosity. Many, but by no means all people undergo profound spiritual experiences involving personal contact with their hidden spiritual essence. These events, which always have ego-death (giving up their struggle for survival), followed by a transcendent rebirth at their core, so transform their lives that they often say they have been born again. Others, after having spent endless, anxious empty hours of futile effort to contact the sacred, certainly experience inner conflict. For them, it is tempting to question one's capability to know God, or that he even exists. Yet, on another level, when these same people ponder the beauties of the architectural, musical, and doctrinal expressions of religious worship, they feel a profound sense of peace and the reassurance of belonging. Which is person is correct? Which is superior?

Hemisity resolves these artificial conflicts. RPs, because of their inherent lower levels of anxiety, often deliberately seek and find personal contact in the realm of the spirit. This profoundly changes their lives. They tend to be drawn to the experientialism of fundamentalism. In contrast, LPs are too anxious to venture deeply in the altered mental states of the spiritual. They are too well defended and thus blocked from engagement. On the other hand, LPs are especially gifted to understand the doctrinal nuances of religion. They also use their musical creativity to worship their external God. They find solace in the ceremony and beauty found in the pageantry of high church worship. Knowledge of hemisty shows that both are perfect. They, need not be enemies, but rather to understand one another. As we will see, RMs founded all of the world's religions. LPs continue to support and defend them.

How Hemisity Can Resolve Conflicts with One's Parents and Brothers and Sisters:

As seen, in Chapter 3 and 6, because of the opposite processing orientations of the right and left hemispheres, RPs and LPs differ considerably in the way they view the world and the way they behave. As a consequence, if one is dealing with a family member of whose hemisity is opposite to you own, their responses to you may be quite different than those of a member of the same hemisity. Thus, it is to be expected that if one's parent is of the same hemisity as oneself, they will be more aligned with you and have expectations compatible with those of your own. If they are different in hemisity than you, you may find their reactions and demands to be somewhat different than yours.

Since in your earlier years, both of your parents will want you to thrive by providing you with food, shelter, and protection, their differences at first will be inconsequential. However, as you grow and develop further, some conflicts may arise. For best development, it would be desirable to have one parent of the same hemisity as your own, and one of the opposite. They each have important contributions to make to your development, as you will need to become well-rounded in your orientation. If both parents are of your same hemisity, you may not be exposed to the opposite but valid points of view and your development may be somewhat one sided. If, on the other hand, your both parents are of opposite hemisity to you, you may feel you were born into an alien family, a complaint I have heard more than once.

Once you learn your own hemisity, and that of your nuclear family members, these conflicts can be understood and resolved. For example, RPs are often more bold, warm and cooperative in their relations, while LPs tend to be more cautious, impersonal and competitive. If you are a RP and your one of your parents is a LP, you may find yourself continually being restrained, disciplined, and seemingly unloved by that parent. However, if your other parent is a RP, you will enjoy their encouragement, warmth, and admiration. Once that you know that your LP parent is only expressing their concern that you should keep away from danger, learn to master your control of things, and develop to be the best, you can appreciate their well-intended contributions to your ultimate growth and well-being. In turn, if you are a LP and one of your parents is a RP, you might find yourself being fondled excessively, expected to attempt fear-invoking challenges, and to intuitively understand how things work. In contrast, your LP parent will be less in your face, more cautioning, and more willing to fill in the details. They each are loving you in their own way.

Further, whether your brother or sister is of the same or different hemisity from yourself can drastically affect your life's experience. Being alike or different in hemisity may influence whether you become the best of friends because of your common attitudes, or the worst of enemies because you don't understand or agree with each other. It would appear best to have a brother or sister whose hemisity is different than your own. That way you are caused to become familiar with an opposite, but equally correct mode of operation. Once you identify your own hemisity and that of your family members, a great clarification occurs. It can bring about a real burst of insight and compassion. This follows as you understand how the other was coming from a bottom-up or top down approach to life that seemed to be in conflict with your own, but was actually complementary. Now you can appreciate and allow for their hemisity needs. Synergy and love often result!

Understanding Hemisity can Improve Relations with Relatives, Friends, and Strangers

Learning to recognize the hemisity of others by their words and behaviors is a very valuable skill. Its mastery can increase benefits and minimize potential harm inherent in normal human relations. Before I had discovered hemisity, when I (RM) was introduced to a new family, I automatically gravitated to the men of the family because the males in my family were dominant. To my embarrassment on some occasions, the men I ended up talking to were neither the boss, nor policy formers of the family. They were merely the loyal supporters of their queen. Thus, it pays to know with whom you are talking.

If one knows whether one is relating to a LP or a RP, one need not waste time pursuing one's own possibly crossed interests with the other. LMs are more fascinated with sports, politics, and business. Unlike RMs, they are usually not interested in discussing their emotions, innovation, radical ideas, or candid self-evaluation. Generally, RPs are inherently more cooperative, independently judging what others know, while LPs tend to form hierarchal competitive gangs, where "It's who you know" that matters. What a difference! Understanding hemisity allows you to bring out the best in others and match it with your own.

Often one must deal with strangers, for example other unknown citizens, store clerks, mechanics, store cashiers, bank tellers, nurses, doctors, or policemen. It is helpful to know whether each is a LP or a RP. You can expect RPs to be more personal, cooperative, and bottom-line oriented, while LPs will be more impersonal, legalistic, and detail oriented. This knowledge can make a big difference in one's approach and how successful the interaction will be. While it is nice to work with a cooperative RP who understands the big picture, the highly detailed orientation of a LP has solved many a problem. Often, the orientation and insights of both are required.

In Guatemala, I have a LM friend (Eduardo) of a RM friend (Roberto), who has chosen to form an ongoing relationship with me (a RM). He is an older architect. He occasionally creates coffee get-togethers for the three of us to chat. Since he always likes to tease, he says things like "if Roberto is late, we can have fun picking his bones before he gets here. That's what we like to do behind the other's back down here." His conduct of our conversations, even when his best friend Roberto is present, are mini duals, like children competing with each other. He is continually looking to "one-up" us, and he has an acute memory that enables him to regularly do so. He would never lower himself to ask a question for information, because that would in his view place him in an inferior position to the other with the information. He delightedly took offense when I mistakenly wrote his name as Edwardo, taking great pains to correct me.

Knowing that I am faithful to my wife, he enjoys inviting interested young women to our table, telling them that a very rich Gringo (Ha!) is over there who is looking for some fun, laughing at my discomfort. When, I mentioned that in England there were more Mortons in the phone book than Smiths, he said "That's Ok, because fortunately I only know one." Being very political, he informs me that he hates all Communists and if there were another local uprising "I'll be there, pushing so it never ends until the last few Commies surrender unconditionally or are exterminated to their final doggish tail-wag."

After a dual purpose motorcycling accident where I lost a couple of toes and damaged my pelvis, he was very faithful in writing me notes to cheer me up, like: "How is that foot-in-your-mouth (excuse me, I meant 'your foot') coming along? Anyway, hope you are recovering OK. Stop putting your foot IN it, and start putting it ON the metaphorical accelerator, Morton!", or "How're your ole' pelvis-and-hips—paraphrasing "fish-and-chips"—doing? Please take notice that your pals fully expect you doing the conga at Hooters in a fortnight or so." As you might recognize, this clever repartee style, so typical of LPs, is quite different than that commonly used by RPs.

RPs are inclusive and work to save the other's face, not to make them look foolish in order to one up them. My RM motorcycle friends were inclusive like family and very congenial. I also had an older LM motorcycle buddy who, while a true friend, could not help being exclusive, demanding to be the leader of the pack for each ride. Any weakness shown by another member during the ride, such as falling, or stalling in the middle of a river, was photographed and subject to playful ridicule to enhance his dominance in conversation at our dinner stops. One of the RM riders in his exasperation, grabbed my LM friend by his helmet chin bar, jerking him around, told him to stop being such a wind bag. My LM friend, was a good person and only acting out his hemisity. Once he rode with me for many miles toward home, protecting me when my clutch cable was broken and I could not stop. Another time when my chain broke and we were hours from home, he produced a missing link from his tool kit and replaced it in my chain, saving the day. He was my hero!

Hemisity Powerfully Influences the Choice of One's Profession

As we shall see next, hemisity influences one's

life path in other ways as well. For example, as a research project we wanted to know what the hemisity of the general population was before any competitive selection into subgroups had occurred. In the US everybody goes to high school, so there is no selection among those students. We measured the hemisity of over one thousand (1049) high school upperclassmen both in Utah and Hawaii. We found, not only almost equal numbers of boys and girls, as expected. But also, importantly, that there were also an equal number of RPs and LPs, which were distributed differently than by sex. This equality in the numbers of RPs and LPs in the general population was an important new finding.

Going on to gain entrance into a state university was another matter. It is competitive. There are standards enforced, which some applicants do not meet. We wondered if this would cause hemisity sorting. When we measured the hemisity of 228 University of Hawaii freshmen, we found that the sorting involved in getting into college resulted in a 1% difference between the number of right and left-brainers at the lower division level. By the time they had reached upper division college courses, this sorting had increased to a 34% difference between rights and lefts in a given course. By the time they had become faculty members, there was up to a 57% difference between the hemisity among these professionals. There also was the large well known sex selection. For example, there were no female mathematics professors. These differences are illustrated in **Table 14** (Table 2 in the original publication).

Thus, RPs were enriched within astronomers, architects, and mechanical engineers, where big picture skills are valuable. In contrast particle physicists, biochemists, and microbiologists were more often enriched in LPs whose micro-detail orientation served them best. Nevertheless, not all astronomers were instrument-using RPs. A few LP instrument-makers thrived as astronomers as well. Similarly among the **Table 14** particle physicists, a few RPs brought a higher order to the many subatomic particles discovered by the LPs. Clearly, no matter what your hemisity, you can make a valuable contribution to your field of interest. However, it helps to know what your hemisity is, and use its strengths to attack problems and find solutions.

Why and how does increasing hemisity sorting accompany higher education or competitive training? A probable explanation is that it resulted from each person being exactly who they are (and are not), doing what they liked to do the best and avoiding that at which they did poorly. That is, in college, one tends to excel more in one area than another. It is important to master the basics, such as the three Rs. However, if one goes beyond that, a selection begins to occur. For example, let's say Arnie is taking several different courses, such a calculus, zoology, history, and literature. At the end of the term, he was punished with poor grades in history and literature, but rewarded by good marks in calculus and zoology. If one

Table 2: Brain hemisphericity distributions within populations of fifteen professions (n=421)

GROUP percent participation	n	LEFT BRAIN	Left Males	Left Females	RIGHT BRAIN	Right Males	Right Females
Unsorted College Entrants	228						
Western Civilization students 62	228	57%	19%	38%	43%	22%	21%
Specialist Populations	422						
Microbiology Professors 74	14	86%*	72%	14%	14%	14%	0%
Biochemistry Professors 95	18	83%*	72%	11%	17%	17%	0%
Physics (particle)Professors 80	15	73%	73%	0%	27%	27%	0%
Philosophy Professors 73	11	73%	54%	19%	27%	27%	0%
Mathematics Professors 93	27	70%	70%	0%	30%	30%	0%
Accountancy Professors 75	9	67%	44%	22%	33%	22%	12%
Law Professors 83	19	63%	32%	31%	37%	21%	16%
Art Professors (vs. Artists) 92	27	63%	38%	25%	37%	29%	8%
Civil Engineering Professors 89	17	53%	53%	0%	47%	41%	6%
Clin. Psychologists (yel. pages) 75	29	52%	24%	28%	48%	28%	20%
Electrical Engineering Profs. 75	16	50%	50%	0%	50%	44%	6%
Physicians (Medical Students) 80	178	49%	25%	24%	51%	26%	25%
Mechanical Engineering Profs. 75	9	44%	33%	11%	56%	56%	0%
Architecture Professors 100	12	33%*	26%	4%	67%	61%	9%
Astronomy Professors 66	21	29%*	30%	0%	71%	60%	10%

* p <0.05.

(yel. pages) = American Psychological Society Members advertising in the yellow pages of the Honolulu phone directory.

(Medical Students): due to extremely low attrition rates of medical students, it was convenient to test them in mass rather than scheduling a separate appointment with each of them after they became clinicians.

125

failed in one course and excelled in another, they could hardly be blamed for proceeding in the direction of their success. In this case, Arnie naturally begins to feel that he likes the sciences better than the humanities. When it is time to enroll for the next round of classes, one finds themselves signing up for more of the courses that they like. Thus, often career specializations tend to match a person's right or left brain-orientations. The sorting results showed RP "Lumpers" successfully pursuing their curiosity about the big picture, and LP "Splitters" successfully pursuing their important detail interests. Thus, one ends up self-selecting topics where one does best and ends up becoming a specialist, be it doctor, lawyer, teacher, government officer, or scientist. Of course, a similar self-selection process often occurs among the working class, where ever there is competition for a job, based upon skill.

These have been a few illustrations of the value in knowing one's hemisity and that of others in living a more friction free, effective life. In the next chapter, pursuing the effect of hemisity on courtship and marriage, familial polarity is discovered. Knowledge of this, com ined with hemisity, can transform one's experience for-ever.

CHAPTER 8: How the Hemisity of Courtship Led to the Discovery of Familial Polarity

After determining the hemisity of thousands of students and faculty within the University of Hawaii, the next question that arose was: What might the hemisity of members of heterosexual couples be? If you think about it, you will notice that there are four possible hemisity couple combinations. Two are complementary: RM-LF, RF-LM, and two are the same-same matches: LM-LF, and RM-RF. I was interested to know whether like-like hemisity partners were more attracted to each other. Or, does the old saying "Opposites Attract" actually apply to the hemisity pair bonding of spouses?

I determined the hemisity of 412 partners of 206 couples who had been together longer than 5 years. The distributions in this unpublished study were as follows: Of the 412 heterosexual partners, by definition 50% were men and 50% were women. In terms of hemisity, there were 53% LPs and 47% RPs, a fairly common distribution. However, among the four possible partner combinations,

40% were LM-RF pairs,
27% were RM-LF pairs,
20% were LM-LF pairs, and
13% were RM-RF pairs.

Thus, 33% (20+13) of the pairs were between partners of like hemisity. In contrast, *twice* as many: 67% (40+27) of the pairs were between partners of opposite (complementary) hemisity. So, the old saying "opposites attract" makes sense in terms of hemisity. We will uncover the deeper meaning of these relationships.

Among the complementary couples (RM-LF or RF-LM), the right brain-oriented partner, male or female, was usually the *de facto* leader of the nuclear family.

Table 15 shows six paired elements from the list of 30 pairs of differences between LPs and RPs, taken from **Table 9** of chapter 3, supporting RP spousal dominance in the home. From these it may be seen that in the RM-LF or LM-RF pairs, the RP was dominant, male or female, as the case may be.

However, in the "same-same" RM-RF pairs, leadership was hotly contested, leading to a relative instability of this pair. In contrast, the LM-LF pairs were the most stable of the four. There, leadership usually fell on the larger, often-unwilling male. Marital dominance is not to be confused with work dominance outside of the home. As mentioned earlier, at work LPs often form highly competitive exclusive "It's who you know" groups in an unconscious attempt to avoid RP domination.

At this point a very important question arose: Might the hemisity of the children from each of the four couples differ, and if so, in what ways? **Figure 6** illustrates findings on offspring hemisity from the four possible hemisity couples. These were based upon 3-5 generation genealogies from 14 unrelated families. Significantly, for the complimentary couples, both the RM-LF pairs, and the LM-RF pairs, hemisity was usually "like father, like son", and "like mother, like daughter". That is, if the father was a RM, then the sons were RMs. If the mother was a LM, then her daughters were the same. Similarly, in families where the father was a LM, the sons were LMs and the daughters were RMs like their mother. It was as if there were two true breeding lineages, one male dominant, which I call Patripolar, and the other female dominant, called Matripolar.

Table 15. Six Spousal Dominance Oriented Items

PAIR-BONDING STYLE*	
LEFT BRAIN	RIGHT BRAIN
Does not read other people's mind very well	Very good at knowing what others are thinking
Avoids talking about their own & other's emotions	Often talks about their and other's emotions
Can tolerate it if their mate defies them in private	Finds it intolerable if mate defies them in private
Likes longer-term, larger rewards of mate's love	Likes daily small reassurances of mate's love
Often feels mate talks too much	Often feels that mate doesn't talk / listen enough
Not a very strict parent, kids tend to defy	Strict, kids obey and work for his/ her approval

*from Table 12, Chapter 1

Figure 6: Hemisity of Children from the Four Types of Hemisity Couples

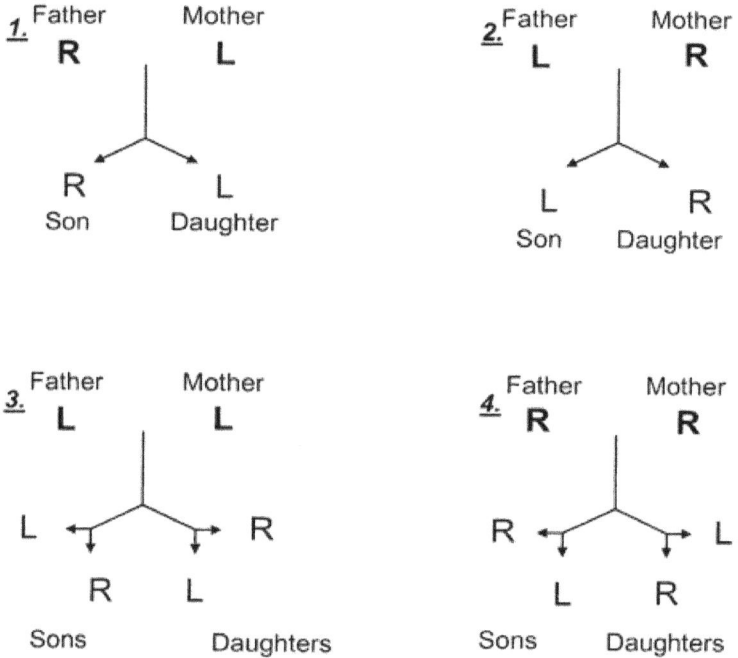

In contrast, for the same-same, RM-RF couples the children's hemisities were random and unrelated to that of the parent of same sex. In a later study, the offspring of LM-LF couples was found to be mostly LPs, possibly because RP infants were lost due to the higher infant mortality that was found for this pair. Children of same-

same parents had high rates of dyslexia and same-sex attraction. This would imply that same-same pairs are hybrids between the two true breeding matripolar and patripolar lineages. As a result, something may have been missing or in excess in utero when the central nervous system was being laid down to cause offspring to be formed with mirror-image type reproductive anomalies. This idea is developed more completely in my book: "Two Human Species Exist" (2012) amazon.com.

Discovery of Familial Polarity

If the hemisity of spouses and their children suggests that there are two true breeding human lineages, this would be a very surprising and important finding. A finding, as will be demonstrated, that would harmonize many presently long-standing, difficult to understand observations about humanity. If so, this would require the invention of a new term to cover this subject. I have chosen to call it Familial Polarity. Familial polarity proposes that there are two pre-racial human lineages, one called Patripolar, composed of RM-LF pairs, and one called Matripolar, composed of RF-LM pairs. Both are true breeding whose children are the same hemisity of the parent of the same sex. In patripolar lineages, the males are dominant in the home and the females are supportive, while in matripolar lineages the females are dominant in the home and the males are supportive.

If familial polarity existed, there should be contrasting differences in courtship and child rearing behaviors. Some of these have now been recognized.

Table 16(here 4) summarizes and compares the currently unrecognized but hauntingly familiar biology-driven opposite behavioral dyads within Familial Polarity courtship and parenting styles. In the patripolar home, the dominant father is a charismatic right-brained big picture husband with a larger corpus callosum. He is assisted by his quiet left-brain, important details, supportive wife with a smaller corpus callosum. As the role model, he sets standards for their children to earn his conditional love. His mate gives them unconditional love and prevents paternal excess.

It is quite the opposite in the matripolar home. There, the mother is a dominant, charismatic right-brained big-picture wife with a larger corpus callosum. She is assisted by a quiet left-brain, important details, supportive husband with a smaller corpus callosum. As the role model, she sets standards for their children to earn her conditional love. Her mate gives them unconditional love and protects them from maternal excess.

In terms of mating behavior, patripolar male athlete or warrior "winners", gaining the stage as heroes, select from among crowds of swooning patripolar female groupies at their feet, as to who will best serve them. However, no self-respecting matripolar female would think of wandering down there. Instead, these women

Table 4: Personality Traits within the Two Polarity Family Types

TRAIT:	PATRIPOLAR FAMILIES		MATRIPOLAR FAMILIES	
Parental Sex	Male	Female	*Female*	*Male*
Hemisity	Right	Left	*Right*	*Left*
Corp. Callos. Size	Larger	Smaller	*Larger*	*Smaller*
Mental Orientation	Big Picture	Important Details	*Big Picture*	*Important Details*
Verbosity, Speech	Charismatic	Quiet, articulate	*Charasmatic*	*Quiet, articulate*
Family Leadership	Most dominant	Most supportive	*Most dominant*	*Most supportive*
Parental Love Type	Conditional	Unconditional	*Conditional*	*Unconditional*
Parental Function	Sets standards	Prevents excess	*Sets standards*	*Prevents excess*
Child's Hemisity	Boys are Rights	Girls are Lefts	Girls are Rights	Boys are Lefts
Parental Status	Role model	Serves the child	*Role model*	*Serves the child*
Mating Behavior	Males select displaying females who are:	Females court winning males who are:	Females select displaying males who are:	Males court winning females who are:
Mating Target	Healthy, intelligent, humorous, loyal, devoted, and want to serve him.	Tall, dark, and handsome, champs winners, strongest. Most socially powerful, richest, smartest of crop	Healthy, intelligent, humorous, loyal, devoted, and want to serve her.	the most physically attractive: leanest, big-breasted. Most socially powerful, richest, and smartest of crop.

take to the stage themselves as a beauty queen. She then chooses whom among the displaying males panting at her feet would serve her best. Thus, the infamous "wardrobe malfunction", where a bare breast was briefly exposed on television at half time of an American Super Bowl football game a few years ago, caused opposite reactions of offended horror or of amusement, depending upon the familial polarity of the viewer.

Further, mature RPs of either polarity tend to be more obese than the thinner LPs. Thus, the matripolar couple stereotype of "Jack Sprat (the skinny husband who) could eat no fat, and his (heavy) wife who could eat no lean. Together they licked the platter clean."

Familial Polarity Antecedents in Other Primates

In modern apes, there appear to be two opposite but little recognized reproductive strategies. In the "patripolar" gorillas and orangutans, the much larger males are dominant and can demand and enforce loyalty from the females of their harems. Thus, essentially all of the children are sired by the harem leader. Young males of reproductive age are excluded from the harem and form bachelor camps where they continually practice their martial arts in anticipation of the day when the dominant male ages or is injured in battle. Only by defeating the ruling male can another male leave their genetic mark upon the offspring of the harem. To accelerate this process, after winning the harem, the new leader usually kills the infants of the former king to accelerate the harem females to come into heat and bear his own children. Essentially all of the children born to his harem were fathered by him.

In dramatic contrast, among the "matripolar" chimpanzees and bonobos, when a female of the troupe comes into heat, she invites sex from any and all males in the camp, having coitus as many as 40 times in a day. This of course results in a huge mixture of sperm in her reproductive tract. It has been found that paternity among these species is random for all the males of the camp, as would be expected. Thus, as opposed to the gorillas and orangutans, where competition for the survival of the fittest occurs at the organism level in the all or none competition between adult males, in the chimpanzees and bonobos apes, it occurs at the cellular level in the great sperm races within the female who is in heat.

This difference in reproductive strategy can be seen in the reproductive organs of the males of the two categories. In the physically overpowering gorilla and orangutan males, only their own sperm is deposited in their non-promiscuous females. Because there is no sperm competition here, the penis of a huge gorilla or orangutan is no more than two inches long. Their testes of both species are very small, being strictly internal in the gorilla. In contrast, the chimpanzee and bonobo males are not much larger in body size than their highly promiscuous females. To deal with sperm competition, their penises are about 5 inches long and their testes are huge, enabling them to release massive numbers of sperm at considerable depth. These apes are not infanticidal. They each must assume that each of the offspring are their own, and are highly supportive of all of them.

It is tempting to speculate that these two contrasting primate reproductive strategies mirror and give biological meaning to the Familial Polarity differences described above for humans. That is, patripolar RMs were the original harem-formers of storied Arabia and matripolar RFs were the ancient queens of Sheba and Minoa. The accuracy of this idea can been assessed as later chapters proceed. So the discovery of hemisity and the determination of the right or left brain-orientation thousands of people from all walks of life has led to a further discovery, that of Familial Polarity. And familial polarity has given understanding and direction to court-ship, marriage, and child rearing.

Figure 7 is a humorous and exaggerated stereotyp-ic comparison of the two Familial Polarities, matripolar above and patripolar below. Individuals from all four subtypes of familial polarity can be highly intelligent and representatives of each have received Nobel prizes for their scientific research. Although the term, Familial Po-larity, is not yet part of our cultural consciousness or vo-cabulary, its existence is easy to detect in the hemisity of public figures, both in politics and in the entertainment world. With a sound understanding of Familial Polarity and a careful assessment of relevant biographic material, it becomes quite possible to assess the right or left brain-orientation of historic figures as well, as previously illus-trated in **Table 11. Table 17** contains an estimation of the Familial Polarity of several families who became fa-miliar to the public through the mass media.

So, on a personal level, once you know your hemi-sity, if unmarried, you will now have a basis for your da-ting endeavors. For example, you can begin to under-stand the underlying biology of why some RM men date certain types of women (RFs) for "hot" sex, but refuse to marry them, choosing rather "a girl just like the (LF) girl that married dear old dad". However, as we

Figure 7. The Two Polarities: Matripolar above and Patripolar below

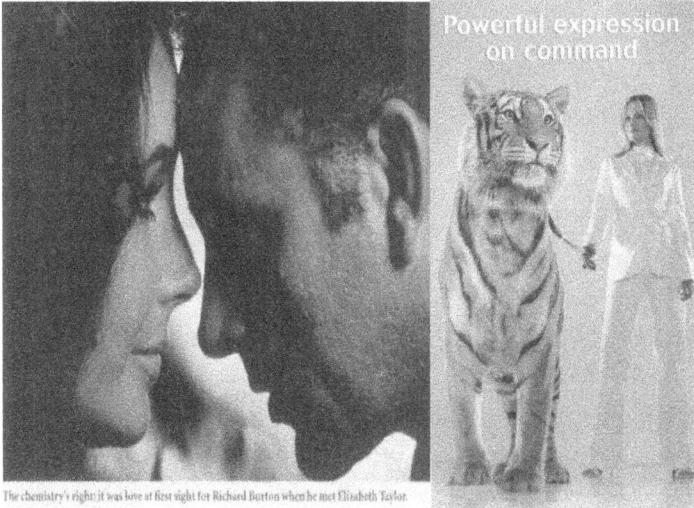

Table 17. Patripolar and Matripolar Public Families in Daily Life
Male Dominant Patripolar Families: Identities:

Bush: George W and Laura	former US President and Wife
Clinton: Bill and Hillary	former US President and Wife
Reagan: Ron and Nancy	former US President and Wife
Kennedy: Jack and Jackie	former US President and Wife
Nixon: Richard and Patricia	former US President and Wife
Irwin: Steve and Terry	"Crocodile Hunter" 2000s TV Adventure series
Fonda: Henry, Peter, Jane	A family of major Hollywood movie stars
"Bunkers": Archie and Edith	"All in the Family" 1970s TV comedy series

Female Dominant Matripolar Families: Identities:

Gore: Al and Tipper	former US Vice President and Wife
Carter: Jimmy and Rosalyn	former US President and Wife
Thatcher: Margaret and Denis	former English Prime Minister / Husband
Meir: Golda and Morris	former Israeli Prime Minister / Husband
Ghandi: Indra and Feroz	former Indian Prime Minister / Husband
Curie: Marie and Pierre	former French Scientists
"Arnaz": Ricky and Lucy	"I Love Lucy" 1950s TV comedy series
"Jefferson": George and Louise	"The Jeffersons" 1980s TV comedy series
"Bundy": Al and Peggy	"Married with Children", 1990s TV series

shall see next, familial polarity goes beyond the personal conflict to affect create global conflict in many profound and historic ways.

CHAPTER 9: The Effects of Hemisity and Familial Polarity on Culture and Religion

Post Ice-Age hominid migrations out of Africa appear to have created human populations of alternating familial polarity striations across the Old World: those that are predominantly patrilinear-patriarchal and those who are matrilineal-matriarchal. As will be shown in this chapter, the former have now been found to contain our RM-LF patripolar hemisity pairs, while the others are composed of RF-LM matripolar pairs. Anciently, small but growing populations of humans were distributed in such a way that these foundational patripolar and matripolar stock striations were usually genetically isolated from each other. One married someone from one's own village, such as the girl next door, thus keeping both lineages pure. However, things changed as populations increased and overlapped into cities. Then one might marry someone from work or elsewhere instead from one's own tribe, often someone of opposite familial polarity. In addition, marauding patripolar barbarians coming from the east on horseback, endlessly raped and pillaged matripolar farmlands. This resulted in the production of large numbers of hybrid offspring, some of which were noted even by Greek and Roman times to be different from the normal human stock in terms of sexual orientation.

Two prescient independent yet parallel syntheses of the prehistory of human conflict were written in the absence of knowledge of familial polarity. In *"The Chal-*

ice and the Blade" and *"Sacred Pleasure"*, Riane Eisler clearly distinguished early female dominant "Gylanic" cultures, which were obviously matripolar in lineage, from the later destructive male dominant "Dominator" cultures, which clearly were patripolar. In *"Saharasia"*, James DeMeo also traced the rise of desert "Armored Patrism", around 4000 BC with the domestication of the horse. Horsemen then began to prey upon the low-violence forest "Unarmored Matrism" cultures of the Old World. With the here-added focus of familial polarity, each of these well-documented theses can be seen to illustrate and clarify further the existence of matripolar and patripolar cultures and their inevitable conflicts. In **Table 18**, a brief summary of earth history since the last Ice Age 14,000 years ago, places these familial polarity conflicts in perspective.

Many contrasting behavioral, historical, cultural, and institutional differences between the familial polarity lineages can be noted. In **Table 19**, ancient behavioral orientations and ecological niches between the patripolar and matripolar humans that have been gathered from much anthropological and archeological data are illustrated. Patripolar RM big-game-killing skills, animal husbandry, nomadic, inventive, and meat-and-potato styles were very different from those of matripolar LMs. The latter preferred the non-violent crafts of the gardener-farmer, vegetarian, settled stable cooperator cultures, where the arts could incubate and develop.

Table 18, The Post Ice Age History of the Current Era.

12,000 BC: Ice recedes, Forests regrow to cover the earth, Present era begins
12,000 BC: Impossible monumental stone megaliths are built by the Unknowns
10,000 BC: Plant abundance leads to unrestricted human population growth and spread

9,900 BC: Oldest continuous tree ring record reaches back to this point in time
9,000 BC: Clovis arrowhead points are left behind in the North America
8,500 BC: Decline of big game in Northern Hemisphere due to overhunting
8,000 BC: Game animals are domesticated: cattle in Africa; goats in Iraq; Herding grows

8,000 BC: Crops are domesticated in Near East: Wheat, barley, lentils: Forests cleared.
7,000 BC: Matripolaric Cooperator civilizations. Unwalled cities, rich in art, technology
6,000 BC: Desertification begins: exploited high pop. areas in Sahara, Arabia, Gobi fail.
5,000 BC: Starvation and battles for limited resources begin. Patries adapt to badlands.

4,500 BC: Patripolar violent reproductive strategy and greater size defeats Matri- males.
4,000 BC: Horse domesticat. by Patris on Ukraine steppes. Nomadic conquests begin.
3,500 BC: Mounted patripolars with metal weapons cross Old World, "Living off the
land", raping, killing, burning, raiding, 'til agriculture was impossible, except in spots.

3,300 BC: Otzi got arrow in neck in Alps:Tattoo acupuncture points on back, copper axe.
3,000 BC: Patries parasitize cultures. Keep themselves separate, install Caste Systems.
       Forests cut for ships & to smelt metal weapons. Moses overgrazes. Desertification.
2,500 BC: Horseback child rearing creates psychoses. Female genital mutilation, Ritual
       Widow murder, Cross-polar hybrids are common, Homosexuality rampant.

1,500 BC: Patripolar Greek Golden Age begins.
  800 BC: Matripolar Roman males suppress females, dominate w. Patri- mercenaries.
   33 BC: RM Jesus is born and the roots of Christianity are laid.

  313 AD: LM Constantine supports Christianity as the religion of the Roman Empire.
  500 AD: Dark Ages millennia of religious domination and cultural stagnation begins.
  622 AD: RM Mohammed founds Islam.

1517 AD: RM Luther, the Protestant Reformation, and European Renaissance begins.
1859 AD: RM Darwin publishes his Origin of the Species.
1915 AD: RM Einstein develops the theory of general relativity.

1945 AD: Atom bombs were dropped on Japan.
1953 AD: DNA structure is published.
2003 AD: Human DNA Genome is sequenced.

Table 19. Patri-and Matripolar Adaptations and Ecological Orientations:

	Patripolar:	Matripolar
Field Specializations:	Early Big-Game Hunters	Gatherers
	Midperiod Herdsmen	Gardeners
	Later Ranchers	Farmers
Species domestication:	Horse, Wheat, Barley	Ox?, Legumes?
Dietary Orientation:	Meat, Blood, Dairy	Vegetarian, Spices
Mobility:	Nomadic, Marginal Land	Stationary, Best land
Group Discipline to Survive:	Yes, Militaristic	No, Laissez faire
Society Types:	Dominator cultures	Cooperator culture
Early Arts Development:	Barbarian Invaders	High Arts-Cultures

The ethnic database of 1170 cultures compiled by George Murdoch in 1967, and scanned for 15 social variables by James DeMeo in 1998, forms the basis for **Table 20**. Obviously, the members of two polarities are quite different in their basic attitudes, behaviors, and social institutions regarding the treatment of children, sexuality, and rights of women. The dominant male patripolars are harsher and more rigid in attitude, possibly to protect their own wife and children from their fellow male's tendencies toward violence toward others. In addition, patripolar nomadism demanded a much tighter familial control in terms of the use of time and resources in order to survive. This was not a child or female indulgent situation, and required much higher discipline and order to survive in the badlands than farmers at the oases needed.

Contrasting comments could be made regarding matripolar gathering, gardening, farming and settlement on rich agricultural land which are inherently much more

Table 20. Contrasting Behaviors, Attitudes, and Social Institutions:
From DeMeo's 15 variable correlations within Murdoch's ethnic database of 1170 cultures

	Patripolar	Matripolar
Infants & Children:	Less indulgence	More indulgence
	Less physical affection	More physical affection
	Infants traumatized	Infants not traumatized
	Painful initiations	Absence of pain in initiation
	Dominated by family	Children's democracies
	Sex-segregated houses	Mixed sex children's houses
Sexuality:	Restrictive, anxious view	Permissive, pleasurable attitude
	Genital mutilations	Absence of genital mutilations
	Female virginity taboo	No female virginity taboo
	Vaginal intercourse taboo	No vaginal intercourse taboos
	Adolescent sex censured	Adolescent sex freely permitted
	Homosexual-Incest taboos	Absence of Homo-Incest tendency
	Concubinage / prostitution	Absence of concubinage /prostitution
Women:	Limits on freedom	More freedom
	Inferior status	Equal status
	Vaginal bleeding taboos	No vaginal blood taboos
	Cannot choose own mate	Can choose own mate
	Cannot divorce at will	Can divorce at will
	Males control fertility	Females control fertility
	Reproduction denigrated	Reproduction celebrated

time consuming and relaxed.

Table 21 highlights similar large differences in the social and religious institutions. The contrasts are dramatic and edifying. Through Familial Polarity we can begin to understand the origins of the wide diversity of human societies and cultures all around us.

Table 21: Contrasting Social and Religious Institutions:
From DeMeo's 15 variable correlations within Murdoch's ethnic database of 1170 cultures

	Patripolar:	Matripolar
Culture, Family	Patrilineal descent	Matrilineal descent
And Social	Patrilocal marital home	Matrilocal marital home
Structure:	Compulsive monogamy	Noncompulsive monogamy
	Often polygamous	Rarely polygamous
	Authoritarian	Democratic
	Heirarchal	Elegantarian
	Political/Econ. Centralism	Work-democratic
	Military specialists/caste	No full time military
	Violent, sadistic	Nonviolent, sadism absent
Ancient	Male/Father oriented	Female/Mother oriented
Religion:	Asceticism, avoidance of pleasure; pain-seeking.	Pleasure welcomed and institutionalized.
	Inhibition, fear of nature	Spontaneity, nature worship
	Male shamen, healers	Male or Female shamen/healers
	Strict behavioral codes	Absence of strict codes

Familial Polarity and the Origins of Judaism:

The following are insights regarding the development of Judaism from the perspective of familial polarity. Biblical Abraham was a successful patripolar herdsman from the city of Ur in the Tigris and Euphrates river valley of Iraq. Taking advantage of a temporary wet period, he migrated with his flocks and herds south into the Palestine. With him, he brought his patriarchal religion, based upon Laws of Hammurabi and the Gilgamesh Epic. In Palestine, Joseph, a favorite son of Jacob, Abraham's grandson, was sold to slave traders traveling to Egypt.

There, Joseph was purchased on the slave block by an upper class Egyptian matripolar RF woman to be her household assistant, and not unexpectedly, her stud. Sexually inexperienced RM Joseph from the patripolar "virginity until marriage" culture spurned her amorous advances. Furious, she had him thrown in jail with a five-year sentence to force him to grow up.

While in an Egyptian prison, Joseph repeatedly demonstrated his right-brain big-picture facility for the interpretation of dreams. This greatly impressed his cellmate, one of the Pharaoh's wine tasters, temporarily jailed due to palace intrigue. Later reinstated, the wine taster became aware of dreams troubling the Pharaoh himself. At the wine taster's recommendation, Joseph is given the opportunity again to apply his skill with symbolism and metaphor. He interpreted Pharaoh's dreams in such a satisfying manner that the monarch ultimately made him Prime Minister. Joseph was made responsible for bringing about his proposed solution to the king's dilemma. Thus, he supervised the building of an extensive grain silo system to store the abundance arising from the "fat years" of temporarily abundant rainfall.

As predicted in the dreams, sometime later the wet period ended and the "lean years" came. The drought decimated Abraham's flocks and herds, which were still in the Levant. To ward off starvation, Abraham's sons traveled to Egypt, by then known to be an abundant source of large stores of food. There, Joe gets the last laugh on his brothers. Later, with his help, his father's family immigrates to Egypt for eight generations. (How many of us today know the names of our ancestors eight generations earlier?) There, during those roughly 300 years, they freely interbred as slaves, and thus appear to have become genetically transformed into matripolars. Thus, they became polar opposites of their still-patripolar Arabian cousins who remained behind. These later could not understand their now matripolar relatives, and grew to hate them to the present day.

It is also relevant that, in addition to the Egyptians of Joseph's days being matripolar, the Persian Iranians of the 50 years of Israel's Babylon Captivity were also matripolar. Be this as it may, it is clear that most Jewish couples today are matripolar RFs-LMs, exhibiting the famous "Jewish Princess" and "Jewish Mother" female dominant syndromes, while most Rabbis are detail- oriented, matripolar LMs, paradoxically still clinging to the many details of their ancient patriarchal religious tradition. These opposing elements of familial polarity have a direct bearing on the present seemingly impossible relations between the matripolar Jews and the patripolar Arabs, and importantly between the matripolar Iranian (Persian) Shiites and the patripolar Arabian Sunnis. These family pairs of opposite familial polarities are as miscible as oil and water. This knowledge could lead to many possible practical solutions to these ancient seemingly intractable conflicts. It would appear that all the founders of the world's religions were patripolar males as outlined in **Table 22.**

Familial Polarity and the Origins of Christianity:
Several lines of evidence suggest that Jesus of Nazareth was a RM, unlike most of his LM

Table 22: The Major World Religions were Founded by Charismatic Patripolar Males:

Judaism: *Abraham:* patripolar – Patriarchal, Jews become matripolar after 300 yrs (eight generations) in Egypt

Christianity: *Jesus;* patripolar, as was the early church and Protestantism. Later, Catholicism amalgamated with Roman worship of sun and the feminine to become matripolar: Mariolatry

Islam: *Mohammed:* patripolar, male dominance in home and government. Persian Shiites are matripolar and often in conflict with patripolar Abrabian Sunis.

Confucianism: *Confucius:* patripolar, male dominant in home and government, Northern Orient

Taoism: *Lao-Tse:* patripolar (North China) and matripolar (South China)

Buddhism: *Gothama:* patripolar and matripolar Segments: Theravada vs. Miyahana Buddhism

Hinduism: *Unknown patripolar Arian*: later Dravidian matripolar engulfment

Jainism: *Vardhamana:* patripolar : no killing, lying, stealing, adultery, or greed

Sikhism: *Nanak:* patripolar

.

contemporaries. He was different. Jesus had cosmology skills that modern RM sons have early, but LMs gain only later. These, he demonstrated at age of twelve to the priests in the temple. His RM nature also showed itself through his emphasis on need for the love of a divine *father*, such as in his "Lord's Prayer".

Neither unwed mother RF Mary, nor her later husband, LM Joseph, could have substituted for the genetic need of Jesus for a dominant RM role model father. Neither would RF Mary have been able to give him the unconditional love RMs need from their LF mothers. Thus, he distanced himself from his family, including Mary and his LM half-brothers. If we were to further deny Mary's "unique in all history" claim of Immaculate Conception, her RM son could only have come from a hidden intimacy with a patripolar male, such as a Roman soldier or an Arab merchant. Jesus' possible RM nature is supported further by his creation and extensive use of politically correct-seeming, right-brain derived metaphorical parables with hidden meanings that broke with tradition: As he said, "He who hath an ear, let him hear". In addition, what would not have been expected from a LM, was his propensity to meditate, his willingness to cry, his emphasis on emotionality in the Sermon on the Mount, and his violent driving of the moneychangers out of the temple. Thus, it is highly probable that Jesus was a RM. Further, based upon information developed in my later book, "Two Human Species Exist" (2012, amazon.com), he was probably dyslexic as well.

By the time of the Aryan Controversy (over the proposed divinity of Jesus) and of the adaptation of Catholic Christianity as the official state church of matripolar Rome, in the fourth century by Constantine, Mary had become "The Mother of God". After the more than a millennium of "Dark Ages" that resulted, the 16th century Protestant Reformation began, thus initiating the modern era. It started in Germany with Martin Luther, a patripolar Catholic priest. Among things Luther protested was the demasculinization of Christianity and the overemphasis of the feminine in the Mariolatry that then existed. His protest, along with that of others, led to the reformation of Christian church, and ultimately to the many of the Protestant denominations of today. Protestantism has had its strongest appeal in patripolar population centers, such as in Germany, Switzerland, Scotland, Northern Ireland, and now in within the Republican US "Bible Belt". These familial polarity distributions will be documented in the next chapter.

Familial Polarity and Religious Conflict

As with any new paradigm, a restructuring of the fabric of knowledge occurs with consequent waves and ripples extending from its epicenter. Examples of such exist, not only in the patripolar Protestant Reformation, but also in the patripolar founding and development of the United States of America. This places a new perspective upon the attempts of charismatic patripolar Puritan, Pilgrim, and Quaker males to escape the tyranny of the "moral majority" present in the established matripolar ethnic blocks of the Old World. That is, they wished to enjoy the freedom of belief and worship, which is never permitted under the religious legalism, censure, and oppression imposed by matripolar males wherever they become unified by their hierarchal territorial dogma.

The American Revolution elaborated this freedom theme further under the leadership of such patripolar males as Benjamin Franklin and Thomas Jefferson. In the Civil War, the patripolar Confederates of the white south who wished secede in order to use slaves in a form of economic competition in spite of the wishes of the national majority, again repeated this drive for separation and freedom.

The founding of the LDS (Mormon) and other patripolar Christian denominations dramatized this patripolar separation-isolation theme. For example, a number of recent US social rebels came from patripolar Seventh-day Adventist, conscientious-objector roots. These include Malcom X, David Koresh, and Lee Malvo. The Mormon-derived patripolar polygamists should not be overlooked, either. Yet, these thematic sub-elements pale in the face of Islamic history and possible "Battle of Armageddon" familial polarity interpretations of current Middle East Conflict.

As a generalization then, it would appear that religion and culture have followed the biology of familial polarity, not vice versa.

CHAPTER 10: Hemisity and Familial Polarity Can Lead to Global Understanding and Peace

Hemisity Sampling Confirms the Existence of Matripolar and Patripolar Populations:

In the author's studies of familial polarity, large amounts of data were obtained from the measurement of hemisity of well over 1000 individuals within the community of the University of Hawaii (UH) at its research campus in Manoa where over 20,000 multiethnic students were enrolled. These preliminary data, tabulated in **Table 23**, indicated that individuals, drawn from specific ethnic or geographic locations of diverse populations of familial polarity, varied greatly in their relative matripolar to patripolar ratios (M/P Ratio). For example, individuals of Germanic, Middle East, or the Northern Orient origins appeared to be predominantly patripolar in composition with correspondingly low M/P Ratios. In contrast, many Southern European and some, but not all Southeast Asian populations appeared to be predominantly matripolar in hemisity, each having high M/P Ratios. These results support earlier approximations of national familial polarity made in this book and would appear to have general validity.

That is, the low M/P Ratios indicate that the following European countries are predominantly Matripolar with RMs and LFs most common: Scotland, Northern Ireland, Germany, Sicily, Hungary, and Egypt. To these could be added Iraq and Palestine. In contrast, Matripolar European countries with high M/P Ratios include:

Table 23: Ethnicity and Polarity of Subjects from the University of Hawaii Community

Country of Origin	Patripolars	Matripolars	M/P Ratio
Scotland	31	1	0.03
Northern Ireland	12	0*	0.08
England	8	44	6
Southern Ireland	3	24	8
French Canada	1	14	14
Western Canada	19	4	0.21
Germany	47	12	0.25
France	3	29	10
Spain	2	32	16
Italy	2	28	14
Sicily	16	0	0.06
Hungary	9	1	0.11
Poland	0	18	18
Russia	2	16	8
American Indians	15	2	0.13
Mexican	3	33	11
Hawaii	51	23	0.45
Samoa	27	5	0.18
Tonga	18	2	0.11
N. Philippines	3	41	14
S. Philippines	18	1	0.06
Okinawa	29	0	0.03
Japan	65	32	0.49
South China Cantonese	3	40	13
North China, Mandrin	50	4	0.11
North Korea	10	2	0.20
South Korea	1	28	14
Thailand	0	11	11
Egypt	11	0	0.09
Israel	2	41	10
Palestine	14	1	0.09
Pakistan	15	1	0.07
Indian Hindu	0	28	14
Indian Seik	12	0	0.08
Bangladeshi	8	2	0.23
Black American	3	49	16
Subjects: n=1089	514 Ps	575 Ms	
Average M/P Ratio			1.12

* = Zero values were arbitrarily assigned the value of one. *Italics = Patripolar*

England, Southern Ireland, France, Spain, Italy, Poland, and Russia. To these can be added Israel, Syria, and Iran.

However, no national population consisted of just one polarity. Yet, even though they were mixed, often one polarity predominated. To understand further the nature of the genetic complexity present within nations, these data, together with extensive ethnographic analysis the familial polarity of the cultures and religions of certain of these sub-populations, have been combined into a preliminary and tentative familial polarity assessment within some of the Old World countries. **Table 24** summarizes this analysis.

Immediately visible is the presence of immiscible, competing matripolar and patripolar population elements with their corresponding cultures and religions. For example the Northern Irish Protestants and the Southern Irish Catholics. Their distribution appears more ancient than current national boundaries. These are the source of continual unrest within each country. Knowing this, the question becomes what can be done to reduce national tensions based upon familial polarity. Clearly ignorance of familial polarity kills.

Familial Polarity Rewrites History

The discovery of the two human lineages of familial polarity has opened a new window, not only for clarifying human origins and history, but also for understanding current global conflict. Patripolar males tend initially to be cooperative, while matripolar males often are competitive. Upon having their cooperativeness spurned, patripolars males turn into implacable foes. Originating

Table 24. Familial Polarity Estimates: Eastern Hemiphere

Country-Location	PATRI-R-bom Ethnicity	POLAR R-bom Religion	MATRI-L-bom Ethnicity	POLAR L-bom Religion
France	Huguenot	Protestant	French	Roman Catholic
Ger-Aust-Swi	Teuton	Protestant	Slav, Mediterr	Roman Catholic
Britain	Scottish	Protestant	English	Episcopal (Cath)
British Isles	Northern Irish	Protestant	Southern Irish	Roman Catholic
Italy	Sicilian-Greek	Greek, Pagan	Italian-Roman	Roman Catholic
Spain	Catalonian	Protestant	Castilian	Roman Catholic
Morocco	Moor	(orig.)	Berber	Animistic
Greece	Greeks	Islamic	Slavs	Greek Orthodox
Russia	Chechnya etc.	Greek Pagan	Russian	East. Orthodox
Yugoslavia	Albanian, etc.	Islamic	Serbia	East. Orthodox
Turkey	Turkish	Islamic	Armenian	East. Orthodox
Israel	Palestinian	Islamic	Jewish	Judaism
Arabia, Iraq, Iran, Syria, Iran Lebanon, Egypt, Af-ghanistan,	Persian Arab, etc.	Islamic	Opposition is	not well tolerated!
Africa	Nilotic hunter-herdsmen, Watutsi's, etc.	Islamic	Bantus Farmers, Hu-tus, etc.	Catholic, pagan
Indian sub-continent	Pakistani, Bangladeshi	Islamic	Indian	Hindu
Southeast Asia	Myanmar	Islamic	Thai,SriLankn	Buddhist
	S.Filipino	Islamic	N. Filipino	Roman Catholic
	Moro	Islamic	Tagalong	
China	Mandarins	Confucianism	Cantonese	Taoism
Korea	North Korea	Confucianism	South Korean	Buddhist
Viet Nam	N Vietnamese	Buddhist	S.Vietnamese	Roman Catholic
Australasia	Aborigines, Polynesians, Papuans	Pagan	Melanesian, Micronesian	Animistic

from ancient sexually dimorphic large hunters, patripolar males often make superior warriors. However, using their technological skills, the matripolar male is also a formidable foe. Ironically, LMs have often hired RMs to protect themselves, as in ancient Rome, or more recently in India, employing the Patripolar Sikhs, or in Great Britain the Patripolar Scots. Thus, there is a long history of conflict between the polaric lineages based upon hemisity, that often continues to this day.

Familial Polarity and the Logic of National Governance Styles: Autocracy vs. Democracy

Fundamental political differences between the naturally different power structure orientations of the two polarities have been a major obstacle to the achievement of stabile mixed polarity societies. In the past, patriarchal harem-forming males not only settled their reproductive rights by physical combat, but also their political leadership. Anciently, the winner of individual combat, and consequently the harem leader, regularly demanded acts of physical submission from each formerly excluded male (from primate bachelor camps of immature males) before allowing him to join his family group. In some modern primates, a submissive genuflection of the subordinate before the alpha male's erect penis is required.

Anciently, as a not too far-fetched suggestion, this essential loyalty step brought the benefits of added male partnership to the patripolar harem while securely protecting the leader's breeding rights by the establishment of an early form of the death penalty: "Touch my women

155

and I'll kill you!" Later, acts of obeisance, that is, pledges of absolute obedience were demanded of all male followers. These then became oaths of allegiance, whereby the follower would swear literally upon the loss of his testicles if he were to disobey the orders of the leader, and that his "testi"mony was true. Such laws and "testi"ments were followed implicitly as long as the leader was in power in the *fatherland*. The leader commonly administered spontaneous "tests" of submission to his followers.

The current existence among educated and intelligent modern patripolar males of a powerful underlying dominance psychology was abundantly demonstrated by the extraordinarily powerful patriarchal top-down autocracies of Adolph Hitler, Mohandas Gandhi, and Saddam Hussein. Their followers obeyed orders as if their life depended upon it. Moralistic criticism on past cases notwithstanding, under such circumstances it would be unthinkable on many levels to disobey the leader chief and indeed such almost never happened.

In contrast, the matripolar path to and style of male leadership is opposite to the patripolar pattern. Thus, matriarchal cultures tend to take the form of a nonviolent democratic commune, where age and wisdom are revered. Originally, all males in the camp nonviolently competed against each other in their courtship of the reproductively dominant female. She selected and retained each of them, but only after receiving their individual submission and pledge of undying love to her and her children in the *motherland*. Because each male potentially had sex with all of females in heat bearing offspring into the clan, each child was viewed as his own. Thus, he was also blood-bonded to the troupe by family loyalty.

While the queen attended to global goals, such as the long-range planning of the camp, a trusted prime minister consort, the temporarily dominant alpha-male, attended the important daily details. He arrived at his tentative conclusions by robust competition with the ideas of the other males in his parliamentary gang. This was an early form of bottom-up democracy. However here, all votes were not equal, but instead each weighted by the member's personal status within the troupe.

Attempts to govern mixed polaric groups, either under *only* autocracy or *only* democracy have resulted in centuries of conflict and hatred, and still are unfortunately underway. However, if patripolar autocratic order and constraint was the original thesis, and matripolar democratic freedom and chaos its antithesis, then the republican-democracies represent the synthesis of the two. Of the more recent solutions to governance of populations of mixed polarity, the presidential two party government of the US, a republican democracy informed from Greek democratic and French Revolution models, has been the most successful in creating a balanced golden mean, at least for brief periods

In the dialectic left "thesis", the citizens and society are represented in the US by the predominantly LM Democratic Party, while at the dialectic right "antithesis", wealthy land owners, businesses, and other vested power interests, are represented by the predominantly RM Republican Party. As both of these legitimate political party orientations fight vigorously for the advantage of their own interests, the pendulum swings back and forth, and the country as a whole staggers down the middle of the road. However, in the end, only the authority of the president and his vice-president can lead them to a useful compromise. This compromise represents the dialectic "synthesis", the golden mean, whereby the nation is guided down the middle road toward optimal survival. In a recent period of unparalleled prosperity, charismatic president Bill Clinton was a RM and vice-president Al Gore was a LM, thus inherently non-charismatic. Now, with knowledge of the existence and effects of familial polarity sub-populations, it becomes theoretically possible logically to design new types of governments that can replace current global conflict with greater cooperation and mutual benefit within and across the polaric cultures.

In the American form of democracy, all votes are equal, including those of the females. This golden mean deviates from both the matripolarhierarchal style of status where no male is equal, and the patripolar style of dominance where women's votes are fused with their husbands. Relevant to the latter is the case of LM former president Jimmy Carter, who with his RF wife, Rosalyn, threatened to leave the patriarchal Baptist Church because of their own belief that women are not naturally subservient to men. This is absolutely the case for matripolars. However, since most Protestants are patripolar (and Republican), many RM Baptist men and, interestingly, their LF women feel the reverse is true.

Occasionally it has been advantageous to become that rare crossover from the opposite side. Thus, RM child-Jesus talking with the LM temple scholars was unusual, as was Islamic sir-named Gandhi as a RM Hindu. Similarly, we have the charismatic RM Kennedy family as Catholics, non-charismatic LM Jimmy Carter as a Baptist, and finally charismatic RM Bill Clinton as a Democrat, stealing fire from the RM Republicans.

Furthermore, to have a charismatic RM patripolar leader includes implicit acceptance of the inherently polygamous biology of a harem leader. Thus, there often will be adoring women with whom he must contend. In this regard, beloved RM president Kennedy (in spite of his lovely LF wife) said he just could not help his ongoing gross promiscuity. Similarly Bill and Hillary Clinton have withstood similar vicissitudes of a patripolar couple. Interestingly, the US presidents who have been rated as the best historically usually were charismatic RMs.

Familial Polarity Conflicts Have Played a Major Role in History

With notable exceptions, the political leadership of both polarities has traditionally been held by males. At familial polarity population interfaces, when their leaders attempted to speak to each other, they often talked past each other, failing to understand. This was because there are two unrecognized different languages in any mother tongue: RP-ese and LP-ese. For example, the question, "What are you doing? What are your intentions?" may be interpreted very differently if asked of a LP than of a RP, often defensively by the former, but more cooperatively by the latter. Thus, from within mankind's present ignorance of familial polarity, well-meaning LPs and RPs often tend to misunderstand each other. Because of opposite value systems, they commonly can disagree, sometimes violently.

For, example, the 1978 Bonn Summit Meetings were held between LP Jimmy Carter of the US and RP Helmut Schmidt, of Germany, to settle issues of mutual interest. Returning from each meeting, reporters on both sides released the debriefing information to the press in their respective countries. Both the Carter and Schmidt teams claimed quite different outcomes resulting from the same meeting. So different, that some of these men became inflamed, calling each other liars. By the time the meetings concluded, these individuals, if not nations, had grown to hold each other in deepest distrust. Yet, they both were teams of sincere, well-meaning allies, each aligned toward many of the same goals.

This illustrates the destabilizing effects that unrecognized polarity differences can produce even during peacetime international government interactions. If by accident, RM Bill Clinton had represented the US at that time, the outcome no doubt would have been much more positive, as it had been for RM Kennedy earlier. This would not be true because Clinton was any better than Carter was, but because the polarities of the two national leaders would have matched and not been crossed. They would both have been speaking the same language: RP-ese, which is considerably different from LP-ese. These two language styles were recognized earlier by Deborah Tannen, but she cast them in a male-female, rather than a hemisity framework.

In earlier less stable situations, such matter-anti matter contacts have led to repeated annihilations. In fact, most of written world history centers on these polaric conflagrations. Such remained as relatively local events of human misery until the advent of the industrial revolution and the beginnings of modern war technology. From then, wars became increasingly massive slaughters on increasingly global levels, leading to the advent of the World Wars. In the First World War, patripolar Germany, Austro-Hungary and Turkey took on matripolar Britain, France, and Russia in clashes of higher mortality than the earth had yet seen.

After these two Giants picked themselves up and licked their millions of wounds, Round 2, the Second World War, followed between with self-same patripolar Axis giants against the same matripolar mortal enemy Allies. However, this time the chaos expanded. While the European Titans were preoccupied in mutual annihilation, patripolar Japan went on a rampage of conquest and subjugation in matripolar areas in Southeast Asia. Fortunately, for the outcomes of both of these world war rounds, a successfully governed, mixed-polarity country (USA) was able to neutralize the champions, but at great cost. Clearly, bringing permanent solutions to these escalating dialectic battles between universal Ying and Yang is of the highest priority. With the explosion of technology and the addition of Islamic and Northern Oriental patripolars to the conflagration, a Round 3 could eliminate humans from the planet!

That the two familial polarities have continued to resist interbreeding even in the present is indicated by the specific locations of repeated global unrest, violence, and genocide. These are usually found between the Eastern Hemisphere familial polarity striations at the immiscible interfaces between two biologically different populations of opposite polarities. Because of the existence of these striations, familial polarity has played an unrecognized roll in global conflict. In many cases, these have been sites of violent conflict for centuries, sometimes for millennia.

Table 25 identifies many of these "Hot Spots of Violence" as recurring global sites of killing or genocide. Amazingly, 20 of 21 (95%) of these sites of repeated unrest were at the interface between populations of opposite familial polarity! That is, matripolar and patripolar soldiers were found to be on opposite sides of the battle lines. For example, the Shia vs. Sunni Islamists; the Jews vs. Palestinians; the Serbs vs. Albanians; the Russians vs. Chechnyans; the Slavs vs. the Germans; the French vs. Germans; the English vs. Scottish; the Southern Irish vs. the Northern Irish; the Spaniards vs. Basques and Moors; the Italians vs. Sicilians; the Indians vs. Pakistanis and Sieks; and the Hutu farmers vs. Watutsi Warriors. This global situation has arisen in our ignorance of Familial Polarity. Such startling observations add a new dimen

Table 25, Modern History: Violence at Interfaces Between Polaric Populations

MATRIPOLARS		PATRIPOLARS
	French **vs.** Germans	
	Russians, Slavs **vs.** Germans	
	Jews **vs.** Germans	
MATRIPOLARS	English **vs.** Scottish	**PATRIPOLARS**
	Southern **vs.** Northern Irish	
FIGHTING FOR	Italians **vs.** Sicilians	FIGHTING FOR
	Spaniards **vs.** Moors	
MOTHERLAND	Spaniards **vs.** Basques	FATHERLAND
	Jews **vs.** Arabs	
	Serbs **vs.** Albanians	
"MOTHER!!!"	Russians **vs.** Chechnians	"FATHER!!!"
	Armenians **vs.** Turks	
"MOTHER !!!"	Indians **vs.** Pakistanis	"FATHER !!!"
	Indians **vs.** Sieks	
"I'M DYING !!! "	Hutu Farmers **vs.** Watutsi Warriors"	
	South **vs.** North Korea	"SAVE ME!!!"
"SAVE ME!!!"	South **vs.** North Vietnam "	
	Philippinos **vs.** Moros	I'M DYING!!!
	Romans **vs.** Greeks	
	*Sri Lankan Sinhalese **vs.** Indian Tamils	

* The one case of these 21 examples of conflict that was not Cross Polar.

sion to achieving the goal of global peace. Certainly these facts can be utilized to enable us to evolve to the next level of human evolution: from the killing of **Figure 8** to nonkilling!

Ironically, the idea of separating familial polarity populations as a solution to national conflict was unwittingly attempted by both RM Adolph Hitler and LM Slobodan Milosevic, each asserting that the mixing of (patripolar)

Figure 8: A History of Endless, Needless, Global Conflict and Slaughter

Matripolar Slavic Cro-Magnons   Patripolar Albanian Neanderthals*

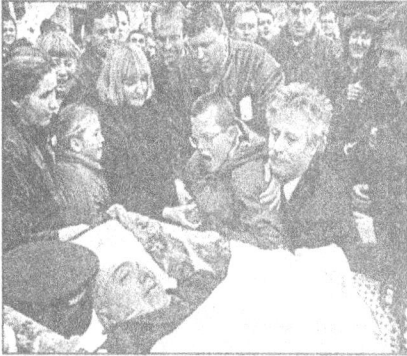

Associated Press
The young son of a Serb policeman, killed in a gun battle with ethnic Albanians, screamed in anguish at his father's funeral yesterday.

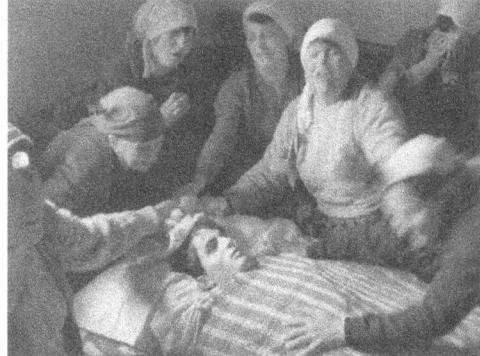

DRAGOBIL, KOSOVO, OCTOBER 24, 1998. A group of ethnic Albanian women weep over the body of Ali Maras Facaraj, a 19 year old Kosovo Liberation Army soldier killed while trying to defuse a Serbian booby trap. [...] developed a systematic method that confirms various types of classifier constructions to verify the accuracy of reports. The narrative, cinematic strategy found that psychiatric patients from individuals who had suffered horrific brutality were unable to describe their experiences in a standard experiential [...]

*Note the prominent brow ridge on the Albanian youth on the right. Ancient Neanderthal caves are nearby.

Aryans or (matripolar) Slavs with other races resulted in inferior hybrid offspring that were homosexual or mentally defective, thus degrading and contaminating the quality of their respective super races. However, they both very incorrectly assumed that their observations of defects among the hybrids was due to the inferiority of the inbreeding race, rather than upon its simple biological incompatibility with their own. This justified Hitler's dehumanizing solution of genocide and Milosevic's of ethnic cleansing, both of which are considered the worst of all leadership behaviors. Further, even if they had managed to separate their polaric populations, this in itself would not have solved their problems. For example, the separation of the patripolar Palestinians from the matripolar Jews has resulted in one of the most long-standing and apparently insoluble conflicts that exists.

It is interesting and important to note that Old World style international conflicts rarely exist in the New World. In the Western Hemisphere, nations are composed of multiple groups of citizens who have Immigrated from many countries of the Eastern Hemisphere. The populations in Canada came from France, England, Germany, and Scotland, native Amerindian, Inuit, and Eskimo stock. In the US major blocks came from England, Ireland, Italy, Germany, Mexico, and Africa. A similar analysis could be done for Central and South America. This multiple ethnicity population structure has eliminated most large ethnic block type national conflicts.

Instead, many of the conflicts in the West occur at the personal level, due to family disintegration. Family breakdown is inherent with greater personal mobility. A son or daughter may leave home to go to the only college they can get into at some other location. They may marry among their new friends there. Upon graduation, they compete for a good job and may have to again migrate and take work at yet another geographic location. Thus, their children grow up far from the original grandparents, often not knowing them and ignorant of their culture.

Commonly, the children seek pleasure and thus create unwed pregnancies, the offspring of which are often neglected and abused, as their parents continue the mating game. Without a home and family, these uneducated urchins are attracted to the power structure of the street where illicit drug sales is the most profitable enterprise. When young, they are recruited into gangs where the rite of membership is murder, often with showy decapitations. From these escape is not possible because their friends will be commanded to kill them. Clearly, this brings us full circle to the savage civilization of our ape ancestors. Family integrity is absolutely critical and must be preserved if civilization is to continue to survive and develop. Yet at the same time, reproduction rates must be brought under control to avoid a population explosion.

Transforming Familial Polarity Conflict into Peaceful Cooperative Complementarity

The discovery of hemisity, not as a sexual difference, but as an individual difference that is based upon one of the two foundational and essential views of reality, brings great utility to living. Furthermore, the combinations of the two hemisities into a marital pairs harmonizes their differences into two vital family units, whose complementary existence and insights have created civilization, but whose differences and misunderstandings have also created endless destructive wars. Now, for the first time, we can eliminate the multilevel ignorance upon which conflict and wars are based and deliberately create an age of harmony. This could bring the greatest optimization of the survival of humanity and its supporting life forms the world has ever seen. To encourage this, **Table 26** illustrates how recognizing the existence of familial

Table 26: Understanding Familial Polarity can Reduce Conflict at Ten Universe Levels

This knowledge:
1. Resolves polarity-based motivation and identity conflicts within **myself**.
    Seeing my polaric identity as perfect, I know that I belong to my global family.
2. Resolves polarity-based conflicts in **my spiritual life**.
    Knowing my hemisity clarifies that my kind of religious experience is normal.
3. Avoids polarity-based conflicts within **my nuclear family**.
    Understanding the polarity needs of each, I can create synergy.
4. Deals with polarity-based conflicts within **my extended family**.
    Recognizing the existence of LP sensitivity and RP intensity removes misunderstandings.
5. Reduces polarity-based conflicts with **my neighbors** (Western Hemisphere) Identifying polarity differences of neighbors helps me to accept them as family again.
6. Avoids polarity-based conflicts within **my community** (Eastern hemisphere). Patripolar and matripolar family groups are inherently different with different needs.
7. Lowers polarity-based conflicts within **my town or city**.
    Unique patripolar and matripolar group strong and weak points become complimentary.
8. Reduces polarity based conflicts within **my state**.
    Dyadic pendulum extremes of opinion become easier to recognize and stabilize.
9. Prevents polarity based conflict within **my nation**.
    Knowledge of reality, the origin and nature of life brings wisdom to social policy.
10. Avoids polarity based international conflict within **my world**.
    Recognition that moving from a selfish national level to a family of nations level transforms competitive politics into a cooperative complimentary global network of peace and prosperity.

polarity and understanding its significance can reduce conflict within each of the ten universe levels.

References:

Gray, J. (1992). *Men are from Mars, women are from Venus, A practical guide for improving communication and getting what you want in your relationships.* Harper Collins, N.Y.

Lakoff, G. (2002). *Moral Politics: How Liberals and Conservatives Think.* University of Chicago Press, Chicago.

McGilchrist, I. (2009). *The master and his emissary, The divided brain and the making of the western world.* Yale University Press, New Haven.

Morton, B.E. (2001). *Large individual differences in minor ear output during dichotic listening.* Brain Cogn., 45, 229–237.

Morton, B.E. (2002). *Outcomes of hemisphericity questionnaires correlate with unilateral dichotic deafness.* Brain Cogn., 49, 63–72.

Morton, B.E. (2003a). *Phased mirror tracing outcomes correlate with several hemispheric measures.* Brain Cogn, 51, 304–394.

Morton, B.E. (2003b). *Two-hand, line-bisection task outcomes correlate with several measuresof hemisphericity.* Brain Cogn., 51, 305–316.

Morton, B.E. (2003c). *Asymmetry Questionnaire outcomes correlate with several hemisphericity measures.* Brain Cogn., 51, 372–374.

Morton, B.E., (2003d). *Hemisphericity of university students and professionals: Evidence for sorting during higher education.* Brain Cogn. 52, 319-325.

Morton, B.E., (2011). *Neuroreality: A scientific religion to restore meaning, or How 7 brain elements create 7 minds and 7 realities.* Megalith Books, Doral, FL.

Morton, B.E., (2012a). *Left and right brain-oriented hemisity subjects show opposite behavioral prefer ences.* Front. Physiol., 3:407.doi:10.3389/ fphys.2012.00407.

Morton, B.E., (2012b). *Two human species exist: Their hybrids are dyslexics, homosexuals, pedophiles, and schizophrenics.* Megalith Books, Doral, FL.

Morton, B. E., (2013). Behavioral laterality of the brain: support for the binary construct of Hemisity. *Front. Psychol. 4:683. doi:10.3389/fpsyg. 2013.00683*

Morton, B.E., Rafto, S.E., (2006). *Corpus callosum size is linked to dichotic deafness and hemisphericity, not sex or handedness.* Brain Cogn, 62, 1-8.

Morton, B.E., Rafto, S.E., (2010). *Behavioral laterality advance: Neuroanatomical evidence for the existence of hemisity.* Personal. Individ. Dif., 49, 34-42.

Morton, B.E., Svard, L., Jensen, J. (2014). *Further Evidence for Hemisity Sorting During Career Specialization..*J. Career Assess., 22, 315-326.

Springer, S.P., & Deutch, G. (1981). *Left Brain, Right Brain: Perspectives from Cognitive Neuroscience,* Freeman, N. Y.

Tannen, D. (1986). *That's not what I meant! How conversational style makes or breaks relationships.* Ballantine Books, N.Y.

Tannen, D. (1990). *You just don't understand, Women*

and men in conversation. Ballantine Books, N.Y.

Tannen, D. (1994). *Talking from 9 to 5, Women and men in the workplace: Language, sex and power*. Avon Books, N.Y.

Word count: 42,215

To test others, scan and copy these questionnaires:

Appendix A: THE POLARITY QUESTIONNAIRE

Professor Bruce E. Morton: University of Hawaii School of Medicine
Published in Brain and Cognition 49, 53-72 (2002).

Name or I.D.#_____. Sex___, Age___, Handedness ____,
Ethnicity of Mother's Parents_____&_____,
Ethnicity of your Father's family_____&_____.

___ 1. When I become upset, after cooling down I don't need to talk, I need to be alone.
___ 2. I tend to be introspective, self-conscious, thin-skinned, and psychological.
___ 3. I would rather maintain and use good old solutions than find new, better ones.

___ 4. I talk more about thoughts, things, or acquaintances than entertainment, sports, or politics.
___ 5. I am comfortable and productive in the presence of disorder and disorganization.
___ 6. I find it very difficult to tolerate when my mate (or important other) becomes defiant to me in private.

___ 7. I don't need a lot of physical contact from my mate.
___ 8. I like daily small reassurances of my mate's love more than monthly large rewards.
___ 9. I tend not to be very romantic or sentimental.

___10. I am more strict than lenient with our children (or I would be if I had children).
___11. Given the opportunity, I am more of an early morning person than a late night person.

Polarity Questionnaire Key:
1. The questions alternate between R and L brain orientations when marked True.
   a. Thus, when odd numbered questions are marked True and even numbered marked False, the result is 11 possible LEFT brain-oriented answers.
   b. Conversely, when even numbered questions are marked T and odd numbered marked F, the result is 11 possible RIGHT brain-oriented answers.
   c. *The questionnaire is scored as* the number of Left brain-oriented answers out of 11: Thus, 1-4 Left answers/11 = Right hemisity, 5 -11/11 Left answers = Left hemisity.

2. Hemisphericity is genetic. You are "either Right, or Left", not a gradation in between.

Appendix B: # THE ASYMMETRY QUESTIONNAIRE

Professor Bruce E. Morton: University of Hawaii School of Medicine
Published in Brain and Cognition 51, 372-374 (2003).

Your Name or Number:_____Sex___Age___Grandparents' Ethnicity_____

For each of these 15 pairs of statements, mark an X at the START of the ONE statement is MOST like you.

Statement A	Statement B
1. I often talk about my and other's feelings of emotion.	I tend to avoid talking about emotional feelings.
2. I am good at finishing projects.	I am a strong starter of projects.
3. I organize parts into the whole (synthetic, creative).	I break the whole into parts (reductive-reductionistic).
4. I am quick-acting in emergency.	I methodically solve problems by process of elimination.
5. I think and listen interactively-vocally, and talk a lot.	I think and listen quietly, keep my talk to a minimum.
6. I don't read other people's mind very well.	I am very good at knowing what others are thinking.
7. I see the big picture (project data beyond, can predict).	I am analytical (stay within the limits of the data).
8. I tend to be independent, hidden, private, & indirect.	I tend to be interdependent, open, public, & direct.
9. I usually design original outfits of clothing.	I dress for success and wear high status clothing.
10. I need to be alone and quiet when upset.	I need closeness and to talk things out when upset.
11. I praise others, and also work for praise from others	I do not praise others, nor need the praise of others.
12. I'm more interested in objects and things.	I tend to be more interested in people and feelings.
13. I seek frank feedback from others.	I avoid seeking evaluation by others.
14. I often feel my mate talks too much.	I feel my mate doesn't talk or listen to me enough.
15. I'm strict, my kids obey me and work for my approval.	I'm not a strict parent, my kids don't obey me well.

L Score = Even As 7 + Odd Bs 8 = 15 Ls / 15 Ls. Right Hemisity =5 or less L answers. Left Hemisity = 6 or more L answers

Appendix C: **Hemisity Questionnaire**

Bruce E. Morton, Ph.D., University of Hawaii School of Medicine

Name or I.D.#_____. Sex___, Age___, Handedness___, Ethnicity of your Mother's family_____, Ethnicity of your Father's family_____.

Write an A or B for the statement most like you, or most like the way you think.

___1. After I have been upset with my mate, **A**. I need to be alone and quiet, vs. **B**. I need closeness and to talk things out. (If you are not currently in such a relationship, imagine how you would feel if you were.)

___2. If my mate defies me in private, I find it to be, **A**. very difficult to tolerate, **B**. something I can put up with.

___3. **A**. I am analytical (stay within the limits of the data), vs. **B**. I see the big picture (predict beyond data).

___4. Regarding disorder, **A**. I am stressed and slowed by it, vs. **B**. I am comfortable or accelerated by it.

___5. **A**. I often feel my mate talks too much, vs. **B**. I feel my mate doesn't talk or listen to me enough.

___6. **A**. I often talk about my and other's feelings of emotion, vs. **B**. I tend to avoid talking about my or other's emotional feelings.

___7. **A**. I tend to be independent, hidden, private, indirect, vs. **B**. I tend to be interdependent, open, public, and direct.

___8. In this country I wish there were, **A**. more high-quality law and order, or **B**. more personal freedom.

___9. **A**. My daydreams are not vivid, vs. **B**. My daydreams are vivid.

___10. **A**. My thinking consists of images, vs. **B**. My thinking often consists of words.

___11. I feel that I am more, **A**. conservative and cautious, vs. **B**. innovative and bold.

___12. As a parent in a nuclear family, I am, **A**. the most dominant spouse, vs. **B**. the most supportive spouse (If not presently in a spousal relationship, imagine that you were in one.)

___13. Can you comfortably carry on a conversation with someone in the same room and with another person on the telephone at the same time? **A**. No, vs. **B**. Yes.

___14. To others my desk might appear to be, **A**. neat, vs. **B**. messy.

___15. When relating to others I would describe myself as, **A**. sensitive, vs. **B**. intense.

___16. In terms of my health, **A**. I am almost never ill, vs. **B**. I catch colds, the flu, etc., rather easily.

___17. If I were to self-medicate with drugs, I would choose, **A**. a depressant such as alcohol or cannabis vs. **B**. a stimulant such as cocaine or amphetamine.

___18. **A**. I often enjoy chatting with others, vs. **B**. I tend to find social chatter to be somewhat annoying.

___19. **A**. I don't read other people's minds very well, vs. **B**. I am good at knowing what others are thinking.

___20. **A**. I tend to take the blame, vs. **B**. I try to avoid taking the blame.

___21. **A**. I avoid deeply experiencing or expressing my emotions because they seem so overwhelming I am afraid I might lose control.
B. I am not afraid to deeply experience and express my emotions because they are not that overwhelming.

Odd As + Even Bs = Left score 21/21. Right hemisity = 8/21 Left answers or less. Left hemisity = 9/21 or more Left answers.

Appendix D. **A BINARY PREFERENCE QUESTIONNAIRE**

Bruce E. Morton, Ph.D., University of Hawaii School of Medicine

Your Name or Number:_____, Sex, M or F___, Handedness, R or L__, Parental Ethnicity____,_____.

For each pair of statements, mark an X by the viewpoint that is most like your own.

Statement A MEMORY PROCESSING **Statement B**

1. I look for differences, separate, and analyze things. I look for similarities, commonalities, and unify things.
2. I organize parts into the whole (synthetic, creative). I break the whole into parts (reductive, reductionistic).
3. I manipulate concepts deductively, see important details. I manipulate contexts inductively, can generalize.
4. I see the big picture (project data beyond, can pred I am analytical (stay within the limits of the data).
5. I symbolize and label things: (a symbol=1000 words). I visualize things: (a picture=1000 words).
6. I imagine, convert concepts into contexts or metaphors. I use logic, convert objects into literal concepts.

TYPE OF CONSCIOUSNESS

7. I thrive in the early morning. I am alert in the late evening.
8. I am good at completing things. I am a strong starter of projects.
9. I can easily concentrate on many things at once. I tend to concentrate on one thing in depth at a time.
10. I am orderly, organized, and deliberate. I am disorganized, disorderly, but fast.
11. I am quick-acting in emergency. I methodically solve problems (process of elimination)
12. I am uncomfortable with chaos, and am slowed by it. I am comfortable with chaos, am accelerated by it.
13. I have good ideas, not all of which are practical. I'm very intuitive, insightful about idea applications.
14. I'm self-conscious, feel guilty, and am a poor performer. I' not self-conscious, have low guilt, & perform well.
15. I don=t read other people=s mind very well. I am very good at knowing what others are thinking.
16. I feel communication is my source of power and support. I feel communication is less important to me.

FEAR, AROUSAL, SENSITIVITY

17. I value tradition, respect authority, and resist change. I am innovative, question authority, and seek change.
18. I am more radical, daring, and experimental. I am more conservative, cautious, and avoiding.
19. I tend not to invade other's boundaries. I may invade other's boundaries.
20. I often talk about my and other feelings of emotion. I tend to avoid talking about emotional feelings.
21. I tend to be independent, hidden, private, and indirect. I can be interdependent, open, public, and direct.
22. I seek frank feedback from others. I avoid seeking evaluation by others.
23. I am comfortable in groups, even adversarial ones. I am uncomfortable in groups, unless loyal friends.
24. I have an out-of-control temper, but it only lasts minutes. I can control my anger but it may last for hours.
25. I need to be alone and quiet when I am upset. I need closeness, to talk things out when I'm upset.
26. I often take responsibility, blame myself, or apologize. I usually avoid taking the blame.
27. I'd rather rationalize a way to be right than be wrong. I'd rather be wrong than rationalize a way to be right.

GENERAL BEHAVIORAL STYLE

28. I think and listen interactively-vocally, and talk a lot. I think and listen quietly, keep my talk to a minimum.
29. I tend to use humor to tease or mock the other person. I often tend to make humor at my own expense.
30. I praise others, and also work for praise from others. I do not praise others, nor need the praise of others.
31. I'm immediate, thick-skinned, no time for self analysis. I'm contemplative, thin skinned, intense self-analysis.
32. I usually design my own outfits of clothing. I dress for success and wear high status clothing.
33. I'm more interested in objects and things. I tend to be more interested in people and feelings.
34. I'm very observant and in touch with my surroundings. I'm often thinking & tend to ignore my surroundings.
35. I often feel my mate talks too much. I feel my mate doesn't talk or listen to me enough.
36. I am the nurturance-requiring member of a couple. I am the more nurturing member of a couple.
37. I am a supportive, highly competitive partner. I am an innovative, directive, yet cooperative partner.
38. I'm strict, my kids obey me, and work for my approval. I'm not a strict parent and my kids don't obey me well.
39. I don't need a lot of physical closeness from my mate. I need lots of physical closeness from my mate.
40. I find it intolerable if my mate defies me in private. I can tolerate it if my mate defies me in private.

APPENDICES

Appendix D. continued:

%Left Score = Odd Statement As 20 + Even Statement Bs 20

$\qquad$ *= 40 Left answers/40*

Right Hemisity = 14/40 or less Left answers.

Left Hemisity = 15/40 or more Left answers.

Index

ABOUT THE AUTHOR

Bruce Eldine Morton, Ph.D., Professor Emeritus at the John A. Burns School of Medicine of the University of Hawaii, was born Southern California in 1938. After Completing the M.S .and Ph.D. degrees in Biochemistry at the University of Wisconsin in 1965, he spent post-doctoral periods as a Research Fellow at Wisconsin's Institute for Enzyme Research, M.I.T., and at Harvard Medical School.

He was hired by the School of Medicine at the University of Hawaii,1969. There he directed a neuroscience research laboratory until long after his "retirement" in 1995. In 1974 Dr. Morton set a world record for distance flown in a hang gilder. He was also active in Gymnastics, SCUBA diving, Wind surfing, Snow boarding, and now Dual Purpose Motorcycle tours of Mayan ruins. Dr. Morton has been a member of many choral societies and was in concert with the Boston Symphony. He also spent sabbaticals at USC, Stanford, and at the University of Michigan. He is a member numerous professional societies including the International Society for Research on Aggression.

In 2014 his eighty fourth publication was: BE Morton, L Svard, and J Jensen, Further Evidence for Hemisity Sorting during Career Specialization, *Journal of Career Assessment*, **22**, 315-326 (2014). His four books: *Neurorealism: A Scientific Religion; Two Human Species Exist; Psychedelic Visions;* and *Beyond Men are from Mars* are available from amazon.com under his name: Bruce Eldine Morton. From his home base in Guatemala, Dr. Morton continues his research on the permanent removal of psychological stress.

He may be contacted at bemorton@hawaii.edu.

His website is http://www2.hawaii.edu/~bemorton.

AUTHOR

BRUCE ELDINE MORTON

www.ingramcontent.com/pod-product-compliance
Lightning Source LLC
Chambersburg PA
CBHW022107280326
41933CB00007B/294